A Guide to the
AVON VALLEY
FOOTPATH

SARAH MOXEY

HALSGROVE

First published in Great Britain in 1997

British Library Cataloguing-in-Publication Date
A CIP record for this title is available from the British Library

ISBN 187444 826 4

HALSGROVE
PUBLISHING, MEDIA AND DISTRIBUTION
Halsgrove House
Lower Moor Way
Tiverton EX16 6SS
Tel: 01884 243242
Fax: 01884 243325

Photographs by Chris Chapleo and Sarah Moxey
Illustrations by Emma Moxey

Front cover: Stream across Vatchers Common, Sopley
Back cover: River Avon north of Christchurch

Printed in Great Britain by Hillman Printers Ltd, Frome

CONTENTS

ACKNOWLEDGMENTS

My thanks go out primarily to my husband Tim, my mentor and my guide, who accompanied me on all my walks and was so encouraging during the long hours of research. Secondly to Marilyn Meeks of Hampshire County Council's Countryside and Community Department, who, when approached with my suggestion that I should write this guide, received it with unexpected enthusiasm. Also to all the countless friends and acquaintances who have listened to my tales and have been prepared to share with me their own enthusiasms and local knowledge.

Special thanks go to:

Mr John Newton, Curator of the Southern Electricity Museum at Christchurch, who shared his knowledge of the National Grid System;

Robert and Barbara Sampson from Harbridge Farm, who took me on their horse drawn wagon to feed the cattle;

Mary Baldwin of the Ringwood Society, who gave up so much of her time to discuss the history of Ringwood;

Tony Light of Fordingbridge History Society;

Rowan Brockhurst of Ringwood and Fordingbridge Ramblers' Association.

Mr Brian Greenland, who owned the Olde Shoppe in Woodgreen and loaned me invaluable information.

Mrs Olive Samuel of Christchurch Local History Society.

The Dean and Chapter of Salisbury Cathedral for allowing me to use a copy of their painting of Salisbury Cathedral by John Constable;

and to my brother, Mr Thomas Sainsbury and his friends Jerry Waters and Derrick Barnes, who were the first people I met who had walked the path – they walked it in one day when they were all over the age of fifty.

INTRODUCTION

The Avon Valley Footpath was opened in May 1992. The tape was cut on the Burgate Suspension Bridge by Councillor Rice, the Chairman of the Hampshire County Council Recreation Committee, in the presence of the Mayor of Salisbury and representatives from the New Forest District Council, Christchurch District Council and Salisbury District Council.

The preliminary route for the footpath had been put forward by Mr Rowan Brockhurst of the Ringwood and Fordingbridge Ramblers' Association, and subsequently improved by the suggestions of other local ramblers' groups. After establishing the route with waymark signs, it was finally completed by Hampshire County Council with the construction of the wooden bridge south of Fordingbridge. The path had been devised to link the two ecclesiastical centres of Salisbury and Christchurch, a distance of 34 miles.

Although it is possible to walk in either direction, this guide follows the river southwards, down the valley from the great cathedral city of Salisbury to the Priory at Christchurch.

It is important to bear in mind that this is primarily a summer walk, as stretches of it can be impassable from December through to May.

The footpath is fascinating both to the historian and to the naturalist. It starts from one of England's most famous cathedral cities and passes through the villages of Odstock, Charlton All Saints, Harbridge, Turmer, Sopley and Burton and the market towns of Downton, Fordingbridge and Ringwood on its way towards the Norman town of Christchurch. The naturalist will find that the way is rich in flora and fauna, crossing as it does the chalk uplands south of Salisbury, the gravel ledges alongside the New Forest and the rich alluvial water meadows dissected by many mill streams and irrigation channels. It is also the haunt of kingfishers and of the rare otter. The route crosses two water meadows which are both sites of special scientific interest.

For those who just enjoy the walk, the route affords some breathtaking views from such high spots as Bishop's Walk, Castle Hill and the ridge above Downton.

KEY TO MAPS

▬▬▬▬	RIVER
══════	ROAD
- - - - -	FOOTPATH
·☏	TELEPHONE
·🚐	BUS STOP
++++	POWER LINES
+++++	RAILWAY
👁	VIEW POINT
C P	CAR PARK
☀	ANCIENT EARTHWORK
▢	COTTAGE
⌂	THATCHED COTTAGE
⬠	PERIOD INN OR FARMHOUSE
🏠	PERIOD HOUSE ON PATH
▬	PERIOD HOUSE AWAY FROM PATH
☁	TREE
)(	BRIDGE
✳	STILE
+	CHURCH
▱	SCHOOL OR FACTORY
☁	LAKE
⛵	SAILING LAKE
≋	FORD

It is intended that the maps give a general indication of the route only and are to be used in conjunction with the appropriate Ordnance Survey Maps.

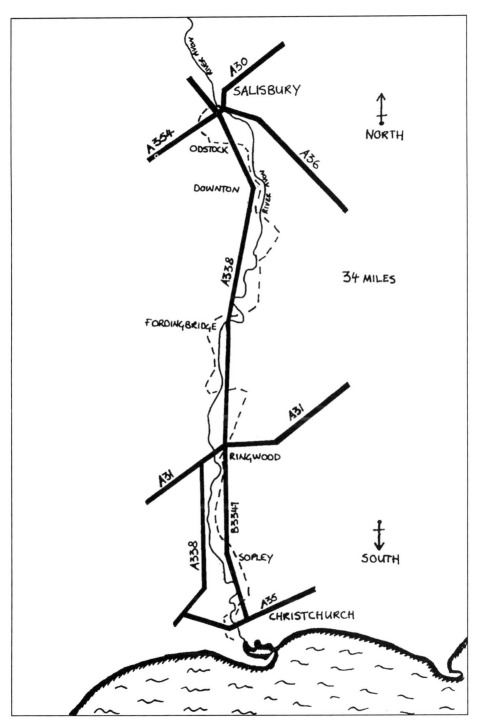

7

Section 1
SALISBURY TO ODSTOCK
4 MILES

All curious travellers that hither come,
Rejoice, extol, and go contented home.

The Avon Valley Footpath sets out from the close of SALISBURY CATHE-
DRAL. Walking through the north gate from the High Street is to enter a
world of spacious green lawns laid out around the cathedral surrounded in turn
by elegant town houses providing a haven of peace and tranquillity from the
hurly-burly life of the town outside. At once you sense the two worlds of
Salisbury, the commercial and ecclesiastical whose history has not always run
smoothly.

In 1075, Bishop Herman started to build a cathedral on the high land above
the River Avon on the site which is now known as OLD SARUM, 2 miles north
of the present city. The cathedral was completed by Bishop Osmund in 1092.
Bishop Osmund was a powerful Norman prelate and also held the post of
Chancellor of England. Using the chapter of Bayeux Cathedral as his guide, he
established the constitution of the English cathedral as we know it today. He
introduced a new order of services known as the Use of Sarum by which the
church of Salisbury became known throughout the land. Bishop Roger de
Mortival, his successor, was also to become very powerful. He was made
Chancellor of England by Henry I and, having fortified the castle of Sarum with
a wall, built more castles at Sherborne, Devizes and Malmesbury. After the
death of Henry I, Bishop Roger supported Stephen, who eventually became
king. However, King Stephen grew wary of Roger's power, had him arrested
and seized all his possessions. These included the castle at Sarum, which was
to remain in royal ownership and thus was to start the enmity between the
Church and the State.

It is said that by the early thirteenth century the relationship between the
keepers of the castle and the canons had declined to such an extent that one
evening, when the canons returned from a Rogationtide procession, they found
that the town gates had been locked against them. At a subsequent meeting, the
bishop and canons discussed these difficulties, together with the other disad-
vantages of their exposed hilltop site – a lack of an adequate water supply, the
cold winds which caused much illness amongst the clergy and the dazzling
white chalk which was very tiresome. They decided to move and to build a
new cathedral away from the castle on a piece of land near to the river which
the Church already owned.

There are various legends concerning the choice and name of the site. It was said that the site was chosen by an archer who stood on the ramparts of Old Sarum and fired an arrow from his bow. Where the arrow fell marked the site of the new cathedral. Another legend suggests that the Virgin Mary appeared to Bishop Richard Poore in a dream and indicated where building should start – this could also be a possible origin for the name of the site, Myrfield or Mary's Field. Other origins of the name could be 'maer' field, as the word maer means boundary and the boundary of three hundreds meet at this point. Alternatively, it could derive from 'marshy', as the site, being at the confluence of five rivers – the Wylye, Avon, Ebble, Nadder and Bourne – is extremely wet. In fact it was so prone to flooding that an eighteenth-century bishop remarked that 'Salisbury is the sink of the Wiltshire plain, The Close is the sink of Salisbury and the Bishop's Palace is the sink of the Close.' Records tell us that in 1635, clergy attending service during a period of flooding had to ride on horseback up the nave to the choir. The last time the cathedral was seriously flooded was in 1915, when the water rose to a depth of 10 inches in the church. This is commemorated by a plaque on the base of the last column on the left of the nave before the transept.

A site having been chosen, the old cathedral was surrendered to the King and the building of a new one commenced in 1220 by Bishop Richard Poore. Work continued for forty years, spanning the reigns of Richard I, John and Henry III, under the control of Canon Elias de Dereham and Nicholas of Ely, the master mason who was probably responsible for much of the design. In 1229 Bishop Richard Poore was transferred to Durham, closely followed by Elias de Dereham, and the building work was continued by Bishop Bingham. The main building was completed by Bishop Giles de Bridport and it was consecrated on 25 March 1260. The spire and west front were not added for about another hundred years.

The town grew during the same period. The land around the cathedral close having been divided into plots of equal size to create a chequer board pattern, each plot known as a chequer. Where possible, the streets were straight and crossed each other at right angles in the way that modern American towns are designed today, but vastly different from medieval towns of the time with their narrow winding lanes. The town was designed around a wide open Market Square and the river water was unusually incorporated into the street design as water was redirected from the Town Mill to run in open canals down the centres of the streets. This brought both drinking and household water straight to the door of each house and provided a ready supply in case of fire, which was a major problem of the day.

The cathedral itself was built almost entirely during the architectural period now known as Early English. It was built of 50,000 tons of Chilmark stone quarried to the west of the town, 3500 tons of oak from the New Forest, and 15,000 tons of Purbeck stone from Worth Matravers used to construct the clusters of pillars to be seen in the nave. After its consecration in 1262, Bishop Walter de la Wyle instigated the building of a detached belfry. Sadly, it no longer exists, as it was demolished by James Wyatt in 1789. At the time, it stood near the present site of Elizabeth Frink's 'Walking Madonna'. Bishop Walter de la Wyle was also responsible for the building of the chapter house and the beautiful cloisters, which are the oldest in the country.

Following the granting of all the stone from the old cathedral for the improvement of the new cathedral by Edward III in 1327, Richard Farleigh designed and built the tower and spire in 1334, which today soars 404 feet above the town and is the tallest spire in Great Britain. At the top is a small casket let into the capstone containing a fragment of cloth believed to be a relic of the Virgin Mary and intended to guard against fire and tempest. The base of the spire is octagonal and here the walls are 2 feet thick, but for the most part they are a mere 9 inches thick and are strengthened internally by the original timber scaffolding. It is still possible to see the old wheel installed to haul building materials to the top of the spire. (It is interesting to note that the spire is 2 feet out of plumb).

The cathedral was described by Celia Fiennes in the 1680s as 'the finest in England in all respects; it only lyes low in a watry meadow so that the foundations is in the water made of faggots and timber, yet notwithstanding its want

Salisbury Cathedral from a painting by John Constable.
Courtesy of the Dean & Chapter of Salisbury Cathedral.

of a riseing ground to stand on, the steeple is seen many miles off, the spire being so high it appears to us below as sharpe as a Dagger.'

If you can spare the time to go inside the cathedral before setting off, you will find that the interior is open and uncluttered, due mainly to the work of the architect James Wyatt, who was engaged by Bishop Shute Barington between 1782 and 1791 to redesign the cathedral. He reorganised the interior, moving many of the monuments and destroying the stained glass windows. Wyatt, who earned the nickname of Destroyer, went on to demolish two chantry chapels and the belfry because it intercepted the most striking view of the cathedral. He was also responsible for the wide sweeping lawns around the cathedral itself; these were laid out when he ordered the removal of the graveyard. Amongst the remaining monuments on the south side of the nave, and of particular interest to the walker or pilgrim is the shrine of Bishop Osmund, who completed the building of the cathedral at Old Sarum in 1092. He died in 1099. His bones were at some point moved to the new cathedral and in 1457 he was canonised. Many miracles are said to have been wrought at his tomb. Down each side of the shrine is a row of three holes through which pilgrims have, over the centuries, thrust their diseased limbs or even their ailing babies, in the hope of a miracle cure.

Elizabeth Frink's 'Walking Madonna'.

Amongst its treasures, the cathedral contains England's oldest working clock, made in 1386, and which once hung in the belfry. It also contains the tomb of William Longespee, a founder of the cathedral who was witness to the signing of the Magna Carta. (One of the four copies in existence today can be seen in the library).

The statue of 'The Walking Madonna' provides a symbolic place for the footpath to start. It stands beside the path leading to the north porch of the cathedral, surrounded by the lawns, majestic trees and elegant houses of the Close. Most of the houses were built at the same time as the cathedral, although many have been altered over the years. The Close was designed, as the town, on a grid plan. Large rectangles were reserved in the centre for the cathedral and the bishop's palace – now the Cathedral School. The roads around the central area crossed at right angles,

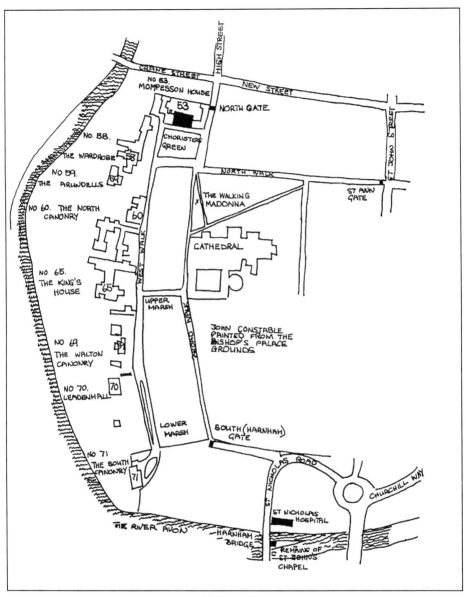

Salisbury Close.

and the houses were built – by those with the right to occupy stalls in the cathedral – on plots of land around the perimeter of the Close. Generally the houses have a similar history; built during the thirteenth century, confiscated by Henry VIII during the Reformation around 1535 and subsequently leased to local wealthy merchants. Many were sold by Parliament during the Common-

View across Choristers Green to Mompesson House.

wealth. They were rebuilt during the years of prosperity after the Restoration. Most of the houses were redesigned during the early 1700s in the style of Wren who, in 1667-68, visited the cathedral at the invitation of Bishop Seth Ward to report on the state of the building. Thus today we have the wonderful examples of classical architecture which make **Salisbury Close** not only the largest, but one of the most beautiful in England.

Many of the houses are now open to the general public, such as Mompesson House, in the north-west corner of the Close behind Choristers Green. It was rebuilt by Charles Mompesson in 1701 in the Wren style and redecorated in 1740. It is now owned by the National Trust and has been described as 'the almost perfect specimen of a small county-town house.'

No. 58, The Wardrobe, originally built as a medieval canonry in 1254. At the time of the Reformation it was named The Warderobe, as it was used as the bishop's storeroom and wardrobe. Since 1979 it has housed the Regimental Museum and as such is open to the public.

No. 59, Arundells, today the home of Edward Heath, was named after the 6th Earl of Arundell who lived here in 1752. Its last ecclesiastical occupant was Leonard Bilson, who was denounced in 1562 for practising magic.

No. 60, The North Canonry was rebuilt in the fifteenth century and its gardens are described as 'the finest in Salisbury and one of the fairest in all England'. They extend down to the river where the Nadder joins the Avon, and at such times as they are open to the public are well worth a visit.

No. 65,The King's House.   Before the Reformation, this house was the Salisbury residence of the Abbot of Sherborne; all that remains of the original medieval house is the porch, the main building dating from the fifteenth century. It was so named because King James I stayed here when he visited Salisbury in 1610 and 1613. In 1785 it was the home of Lt Gen. Henry Shrapnel, the inventor of the explosive shell bearing his name. Today it houses the Salisbury and South Wiltshire Museum.

No. 69, Walton Canonry, rebuilt in 1720, is named after Canon Walton, the son of the famous author Isaak Walton, who wrote *The Compleat Angler*.

No. 70, Leadenhall. The original house on this site was built by Elias de Dereham for his own use and as a model for the other canonical houses. Its name, which dates back to 1305, implies that it was the only house to have a hall with a lead roof. The present house dates from 1700, and in the 1800s it was occupied by Archdeacon Fisher, who was a great friend of the painter John Constable, who often came to stay here and painted many fine views of the Cathedral.

No. 71, the South Canonry, rebuilt in 1778, is the present home of the Bishop of Salisbury.

The houses can all be viewed across the lawns as one follows the Avon Valley Path along the Broad Walk past the west front of the cathedral.

The West Front was built at a later date than the main body of the cathedral and is much more decorated. It takes the form of a vast screen with statues arranged in five tiers. The great west window above contains all the stained glass salvaged from the destruction carried out by the architect James Wyatt.

The footpath continues beyond the cathedral along a tree-lined gravel drive to the most southerly point of the walls which surround the Close on three sides, the fourth side being bounded by the river. They were built in 1327 by Bishop Roger de Mortival at a time when relations between the church and the town were unstable following the levying of taxes upon the townspeople. Permission was granted by Edward III to fortify the Close and to re-use stone from Old Sarum. There are three gates in the wall; North Gate, which leads to the High Street, St Ann's Gate leading east to Exeter Street, and South Gate or **Harnham Gate**, through which the Avon Valley Footpath passes to De Vaux Place. It was built in the middle of the fourteenth century as a platform over a deep arch originally protected by a crenellated parapet extending on the south side.

During the Civil War in 1645, when Ludlow, the Parliamentary general who held the city against the Royalists, eventually came under attack, he left a small body of men to defend the Close from the apparent safety of the belfry while he and his men retreated through the Harnham Gate and across Harnham Bridge to Odstock.

The gate is bounded by three small houses built during the mid-eighteenth century. Two were built as dwellings for lay vicars, but no. 73, which originally

Harnham Gate.

was the Close Pound and later kennels for hounds, was built in 1713 by a local gunsmith.

The Close gates are kept locked at night; the time of opening in the morning varies with the time of year, as given on a board at the gate.

Passing through the gate, the path continues along **De Vaux Place** between rows of terraced cottages. At the junction with St Nicholas Road, the corner house on the right built in 1542 may once have been the lodge house to De Vaux College, which was built here in 1260 by Bishop Giles de Bridport as a rival university to Oxford. The papal legate, Otho, had been insulted during a visit to Oxford, and in 1238 an interdict was laid on the city; this led to riots and other disturbances, so many students were looking for an alternative place of learning. It was named after the French Valli Scholares Community, which accommodated scholars fleeing from Paris. However, with the restoration of peace at Oxford and the creation of Bishop Wykeham's School at Winchester, the attendance at Salisbury diminished until it was abandoned totally during the reign of Henry VIII. Some ruins still existed until the early nineteenth century when the site was cleared; now only a few stones are still visible, built into the walls of De Vaux Place.

Turn right into St Nicholas Road, and after about 75 yds the **Community of St Nicholas Hospital** will be seen on the left. It was one of two medieval hospitals in the city and was founded by Bishop Bingham in 1245 to provide food, shelter and prayer for those sick travellers who wished to enter the town. By 1320 the hospital had abandoned its healing role and by the fifteenth century it had become almshouses. In 1610 James I granted it a constitution to maintain 12 sick or elderly persons of either sex, to be looked after until their death by a chaplain and a master. This continues today and the hospital is now a retirement home run by a retired clergyman. Of the original building, only the eastern end and southern section remain.

Following his visit to Salisbury in 1851, Anthony Trollope included reference to St Nicholas Hospital in his first novel of the Barchester series, *The Warden*, calling it Hiram's Hospital.

St Nicholas hospital.

The staff were also made responsible for the maintenance of the newly built **Harnham Bridge** and the bridge chapel of St John. These were built by Bishop Bingham in 1245, taking advantage of the recent charter granted by Henry III by which the bishops could alter the roads. At the time there were only two roads crossing the town, the Winchester–Wilton Road and the Old Sarum to Aegel's Ford Road. Old Sarum was the hub of a network of Roman roads leading to the Mendips, Mildenhall, Silchester, Winchester and Dorchester via Wilton. Bishop Bingham realised that to make the new town of Salisbury prosper as a market town, it was important to attract visitors and trade, and it was therefore necessary to divert travellers away from the old centres of Sarum and Wilton. The most important road was the road from London to Exeter which crossed the River Ebble at Bull Bridge in Wilton. Bishop Bingham decided to build a bridge at Aegel's Ford, which became known as Aylewade Bridge and later as Harnham Bridge. This diverted the main London road through Clarendon Forest to Salisbury along Exeter Road and across Harnham Bridge ; it then continued up Harnham Hill and west along Shaston Drove. He ordered the diverting of the force of the river by cutting an additional channel, thus creating an artificial island upon which he had built the **Chapel of St John**. Remains of this chapel are still visible between the hospital and the bridge. Although it has been converted into a house, the lancet windows are still visible, especially below road level. These chapels, which were once built beside most medieval bridges, are now extremely rare.

From 1496, on Midsummer's Eve, members of the Tailors' Guild would celebrate the Vigil of St John the Baptist with a pageant and a procession to the chapel, with a giant representing St Christopher. Running around him would be his page on a hobby horse, called Hob Nob. Although the practice has since lapsed, it is still possible to see Hob Nob, the last giant used, in the Salisbury and South Wiltshire Museum.

The building of the bridge was a very successful move and marked the turning point in the fortunes of the city. Leland wrote in the 1540s, 'The changing of this way was the total cause of the ruine of Old Saresbyri and Wiltoun. For afore this Wiltoun had a 12 paroch chirches or more and was the hedde town of Wileshir.' By Stuart times, Salisbury was the hub of six roads and at its height was England's ninth ranking provincial town.

Harnham Bridge crosses the River Avon, or 'Afene' as it was named by the Saxons, just below the confluence of the Avon and the Nadder. It is 60 miles from its source near Marlborough to the harbour mouth at Christchurch. Joined by four other rivers at Salisbury, the Wylye, Nadder, Ebble and Bourne and numerous small streams it drains a total of 666 square miles. It is primarily a chalk river, and with its clear water is renowned for trout, pike and salmon and was once considered the best coarse fishing river in Britain.

In 1623 the Water Poet, John Taylor, wrote an account of a journey he made from London following the south coast to Christchurch in a wherry, accompanied by four friends. From Christchurch he was rowed up the river to Salisbury. He wrote that the journey up river took one day and he was greeted with a fanfare of trumpets in Ringwood. At Hale Sir Thomas Penruddock rowed out to greet him and at Longford Castle he was entertained by Lord Dundalk, captain of Hurst Castle. He describes his journey as being 'for the discovery of the sands, flats, depths, shoales, mills and weares, which are impediments and lets, whereby the river is not navigable from Christchurch, or the sea to Salisbury.' John Taylor saw the need to clear the river and to make it navigable as far as Salisbury in order to increase the prosperity of the town. Everywhere he went he spoke and later wrote that 'with some change [the Avon] may be made as passable as the River Thames is upwards from Brentford to Windsor, or beyond it; the shallow places in it are not many, the mills need not be removed, as for weares, no doubt but they may be conscience be compounded for.'

In the 1660s, during the reign of Charles II , the Earl of Clarendon engaged a London hydrographer, Captain Yarranton, to produce a feasibility study on making the river navigable. He, like John Taylor before him, saw the river's potential and produced a favourable report. He suggested that the harbour at Christchurch could be enlarged to accommodate 50 to 60 frigates and a ship-building industry, using timber brought down the river from the New Forest. Hengistbury Head could become a fortress with 100,000 men. He also suggested that forges could be set up in Ringwood to make guns for the Navy, using iron ore from Hengistbury and timber from the New Forest. Soon after the report was made, the Earl of Clarendon had to flee from the country to the Continent, but Bishop Seth Ward took up the idea. He raised a subscription amongst the local citizens, as well as making a large donation himself, and in 1675 work began. The bishop dug the first spit near Longford Castle. In all, approximately 300 men were employed on digging shallows and altering bridges, until work slowed down due to shortage of money. In 1677 a group of businessmen formed a company to provide money to continue work on the scheme. By 1724 their venture was abandoned on account of lack of funds, poor management and the problems encountered with other river users, such as the fishermen, millers and the carters who in competition built carriage ways on either side of the river to transport goods by road. It was also found that the building of locks and weirs to enable the barges to travel up river against the strong current, such as the one just down river from Harnham Bridge, increased the likelihood of flooding. After this time there was only a little local traffic on the river; there are reports in 1730 of barges being used at Downton, and in 1753 Dr Pope mentions vessels coming up river to Harnham.

After crossing the bridge, bear right along Harnham Road past the Rose and Crown hotel; this half-timbered building dates from the fourteenth century. A stop here for refreshment or an overnight stay is recommended, as the view across the river to the cathedral from the riverside lawns is glorious.

Opposite is a terrace of picturesque thatched cottages with most unusual step-like thatched porches supported by two tree trunks apiece.

On the outskirts of Salisbury the path continues along **Bishop's Walk** around Harnham Slope. It is thought this was once the path from Bishop's Mill to Harnham Hill. It was given to the people of Salisbury by Bishop Wordsworth in 1885. This path is cool and shady in the summer, passing around a wooded slope beneath beech and sycamore trees. During the winter when the trees are bare, there are fine views across Salisbury to Old Sarum on the distant hillside. Bishop Wordsworth, the great-nephew of the poet William Wordsworth, was interested in local and natural history and founded the Bishop Wordsworth School in the city.

The Bishop's Walk leads up to **Harnham Hill**, and from the top looking west it is possible to make out the stands of **Salisbury Racecourse**.

The racecourse dates back to 1630, when the Second Earl of Pembroke presented a silver bell to the city. This was converted into a cup for which horses would compete annually. There were two point-to-point races. One race was over a distance of 14 miles from Whitesheet Hill in the west to Harnham Hill droveway. The other race was run over a distance of 4 miles from a point near Broad Chalke to Hare Warren, the finish being a point now covered by the present grandstand.

The footpath turns right onto Ashton Drove. Once this drove was marked with milestones, a notion revived by the Earl of Pembroke from the Romans' idea. Beside each milestone was planted a marker lime tree. These trees have disappeared over time. The way dates back to the Bronze Age, when it was known as the Herepath, and later in Saxon times as the Cloven Way, which followed the ridge east to west across Wessex high up above the flood plain. It was crossed near the racecourse by the White Way or Wilton Way, which went south to Damerham and the Roman road known as Ackling Dyke, which went from Old Sarum to Dorchester.

Drove roads were the earliest pre-Roman roads to cross Wessex. From the Middle Ages until the coming of the railways they became increasingly important for the movement of livestock. By the sixteenth century the populations of most cities had outgrown their local supply of meat and herds of animals were brought from the west to supply these markets. It is reported that flocks of between 200 and 200,000 sheep were brought along **Shaston Drove** from the hillsides of Wales to the pasture land of Hampshire and Wiltshire to be fattened before moving on to the markets of London and the South East. It was important that the animals arrived in good health, so to protect their hooves the cattle were shod and geese were made to run through a mixture of sand, sawdust and tar before setting off.

The drove roads became increasingly busy with waggons and pack horses as well as herds of animals, until during the reigns of Mary and Elizabeth I a system of licensing was introduced to control the number of drovers. Licences

View from Dogdean Farm.

were issued to men over the age of thirty who were both married and house-holders. The drovers soon acquired the status of respectable men who could be trusted with the carrying of messages. As they had no need to carry money, they were not attacked by highwaymen, and in time were entrusted with the carrying of promissory notes; this became a system of credit and eventually they were seen as travelling bankers.

Walking down Shaston Drove towards the south, the Avon Valley footpath crosses over the A354. This road came into existence after the building of Harnham Bridge. It became the main road from London to the West of England, replacing the old Roman road, and was described by Leland in 1540 as 'A great Royal Road'. It was used by King George III when he visited Weymouth and was turnpiked completely by 1835 to pay for its upkeep.

Across the main road the footpath continues along a wide grass track between hedges of hawthorn, blackthorn and elder. There are many green ways such as this alongside ancient drove roads; they were known as drove closes or drove ends, along which sheep or cattle were driven to the downland pasture or to the local market. Sometimes they were lanes where a plough team could turn into open fields. Throughout the year they provided regular grazing land for horses, cattle and pigs. As part of the upkeep of these green ways, the tenant farmers who used them had to contribute to the cost of the mole catchers who worked along their length.

Turn right off this green way and the path crosses the open chalk downland of Homington Down towards Dogdean Farm. As the path drops down into the valley of the River Ebble, there is a panoramic view across Odstock Down and the tree-covered hillside that is Odstock Copse.

This copse covers an area of 10 acres; in one corner nearest Odstock village is a small ancient fortification. Today it is obscured by the trees, but a glimpse inside the wood in spring will reveal a colourful display of bluebells, orchids and wood anemones.

In the valley the path crosses another green way before continuing onto the water meadows. In February the hedgerows are alive with small birds, especially the smallest of all, the wren, with its exquisite song. The valley and river banks are carpeted with snowdrops and across the meadows foxes can often be seen or heard, with their russet coats and white tipped tails.

The footpath crosses the River Ebble and continues across the fields to Odstock village, where the Yew Tree pub, just to the left of the path, is renowned for its good food and accommodation.

Looking to the left or north, away up on the sky line can be seen the outline of the chimney and buildings of Odstock Hospital, recently upgraded to become the new Salisbury General Hospital. It was built by the American Army in 1944 to provide medical treatment for casualties from the D-Day invasion. After the War it was converted for civilian use. For many years its burns, plastic surgery and spinal injuries units have enjoyed an international reputation.

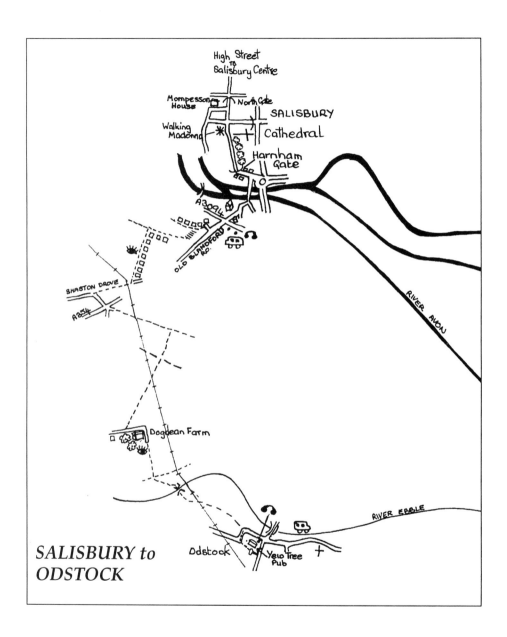

High Street
to
Salisbury Centre

Mompesson
House

North Gate

SALISBURY

Cathedral

Walking
Madonna

Harnham
Gate

A3094

OLD BLANDFORD RD.

SHASTON DROVE

A354

RIVER AVON

Dogdean Farm

RIVER EBBLE

Odstock

Yew Tree
Pub

SALISBURY to
ODSTOCK

22

SALISBURY to ODSTOCK
4 MILES

Maps
OS Outdoor Leisure Map 22
New Forest OS Pathfinder sheets 1262 and 1282

Public Transport
National Rail Station services from:
Southampton via Eastleigh
Winchester via Eastleigh
London via Basingstoke and Andover
Exeter
Tel. (0345) 484950

Bus service from:
Winchester to Salisbury 68
Southampton, X7
Romsey, 34
Ringwood, Bournemouth and Poole, X3
Weymouth and Blandford, 184
Bath and Bristol, X4
Marlborough, 5, 6
Basingstoke, 76
Lyminton X31
Fordingbridge 38

Wilts and Dorset Buses Tel. Salisbury (01722) 336855

Where to Park
Large car parks in the centre of Salisbury

Where to Stay
Free accommodation list from the Tourist Information Office, Fish Row,
Salisbury Tel. (01722) 334956
Youth Hostel, Milford Hill House, Milford Hill, Salisbury Tel (01722) 327572
The Rose and Crown, Harnham Tel. (01722) 399955. Freefone 0800 289330.
Fax (01722) 339816
The Yew Tree Inn, Odstock Tel. (01722) 329786

Where to Eat
Large number of restaurants, pubs, bakeries and take-away food shops in
Salisbury

The Rose and Crown Hotel, Harnham
The Yew Tree Inn, Odstock

Places to Visit
Mompesson House, National Trust
Salisbury Cathedral
Salisbury and South Wiltshire Museum

Directions
The Avon Valley Path starts or finishes at the west door of Salisbury Cathedral,
which is also the start or finish point of the Clarendon Way.

From the west door, follow Broad Walk South, towards the south (Harnham)
gate. Passing through the gate walk to the junction with St Nicholas Road and
turn right towards Harnham Bridge. Cross over the bridge at the junction with
Ayleswade Road, bear right and continue along Harnham Road, passing the
Rose and Crown Hotel. Continue to the junction with New Harnham Road.

Cross the main road and turn left almost immediately, then walk up Old
Blandford Road (keep to the right hand pavement for approximately 200 yds).
Turn right into Grasmere Close and immediately turn left to follow the path
around the back of the housing estate. Follow waymarks and after 50 yds turn
left up a flight of steps to reach Bishop's Walk to the right which curves round
the side of the hill following the line of gardens on the left. After $^1/_4$ mile pass
a stone commemorating Bishop Wordsworth and continue to the end of the
housing, where open country begins. Take a path to the left through a squeeze
stile and head south uphill for a quarter of a mile following gardens on the left
and fields on the right.

At the end of the path turn right (west) onto an old grass track, passing under
the power lines. After approximately 200 yds, the track meets an unmetalled
road. Turn left and walk south-east to the A354 Salisbury–Blandford Road.
Cross the main road carefully onto a wide grass track . Continue along the track
between hedges and after $^1/_3$ mile turn right onto a footpath to the south-west
over a stile and follow the field boundary to the metalled farm road which leads
to Dogdean Farm. Turn left (east) along this road towards the farm buildings.

Pass along the left side of the farm buildings, then right at the corner to head
south. Continue on the grass track around the farm garden and down between
the fields into the river valley. At the stile, turn right onto a grass track and
immediately left over the second stile into the water meadows. Cross the field
diagonally left to a stile, follow the river bank downstream to a stile beside a
wooden footbridge over an old brick sluice gate. Cross this and proceed to the
next footbridge and follow the right bank back upstream for 100 yds to a stile.
Cross this stile, turn left (east) and cross the field towards Odstock village.

Walk under the power lines and continue towards Odstock village over
pasture land until exiting from the field through a metal field gate and turn

24

right. Cutting across the corner of the field go through the next gate. Cross this field following the left hand field boundary to a field gate beside a stile leading onto the road to Odstock. Turn right (south) along the road for 20 yds to a sharp right-hand bend. On the left is a stile beside a gate; cross the stile into this field and follow the left-hand boundary (heading east) to the stile into the sports field and car park. The lane from the car park leads to the road into the village and a good pub for refreshments, the Yew Tree, which is very close on the left.

Section 2
ODSTOCK TO DOWNTON
4 MILES

A Spring eternal – meadows ever green;
Through which in smooth meanders Avon flows,
And pays a double tribute as it goes.

It is difficult to appreciate the beauty of Odstock from the footpath as it passes some way to the south of the village. There are some fine old houses; the first one visible from the path on approaching the village is Glebe House, built as a timber-framed house in the early seventeenth century. The Yew Tree pub, where refreshments and accommodation are available, is an eighteenth-century thatched inn. The Manor House, which can be seen from the footpath to the rear, was built during the seventeenth century; the builder was influenced by the houses in Salisbury Close.

In St Mary's churchyard the grave of Joshua Scamp lies half hidden by a rambler rose. Joshua was a gypsy hanged in 1830 in Salisbury for the theft of a horse. He was reputedly not guilty, but went to the scaffold for the sake of his daughter, whose husband had committed the crime. For many years after his death, gypsies came to his grave on the anniversary of his death. Eventually the villagers grew impatient with the drinking and carousing and decided to lock the church to keep them out. Following this, the queen of the gypsies laid a curse on the village church and pronounced that anyone connected with the locking of the church door then or at any time in the future would perish within the year. It is said that the villagers who were responsible for the deed all died within the year. A few years later the church was locked again and apparently the person responsible also died within a year. After this incident it was decided that the church would never be locked again, and to make sure it did not happen, even accidentally, a ceremony was held to throw the key into the River Ebble. The church has been kept locked since 1995, after first taking the precaution of having it exorcised. At the time of writing the exorcism appears to have been successful.

The path crosses Nunton Drove and passes to the south of the village of **Nunton**. If at this point the reader feels the need of refreshment, the Radnor Arms may be found on a short detour from the walk.

Nunton developed as a thirteenth century demesne farm and a medieval cluster of tenants' farmsteads round the chapel and mill in the manor of Downton. The church was designed by T.H. Wyatt in 1854.

From Nunton, the path continues along Shelve Lane, skirting Bodenham

St Mary's churchyard at Odstock with the rose covered tombstone of Joshua Scamp.

Plantation, at the end of which it crosses the Saxon Way leading from Clearbury Hill to Pepperbox Hill. This green way leads down between ancient yews and ash trees to the A338. The Avon Valley Footpath also crosses the main Ringwood to Salisbury road, but to the south of the old Saxon crossing. From this elevated point it is possible to look across to the opposite side of the valley to the spire of St Mary's Church nestling in the trees at **Alderbury**. On the horizon, cars catch the sunlight as they pass on the main Salisbury to Cadnam Road climbing up over Witherington Down to Pepperbox Hill.

The landscape reflects the interest taken in it by the 2nd Earl of Radnor. He was responsible for planting at least 3000 trees on his land, including Bodenham Plantation, between 1776 and 1828. Many seeds were sent from America by the English journalist, Cobbett. In an effort to preserve the rural life of England Cobbett wrote the now famous *Rural Rides*.

The footpath bypasses Longford Castle, the home of the present Earl of Radnor, but passes through the Longford estate to a shady lane set on a ledge just above the flood plain of the river. The lane, known locally as Love Lane, was once the main road from Salisbury to Downton. It passes through a tunnel of high hazels until it opens out to reveal the wet pastureland overlooked by the unique octagonal Round House and opposite, about 50 yds further on, is the large Victorian brick-built Matrimony Farmhouse.

On either side of the Round House willows are grown under contract to be cut in October for the making of cricket bats. The house itself is a curiosity and

Matrimony Farmhouse.

was probably built between 1807 and 1837 as a landscape feature visible from Longford Castle. It was later extended and converted into the original Matrimony Farmhouse, to be given as part of a marriage settlement. In 1888 a new farmhouse was built across the road, replacing the old, and its outbuildings were converted into living accommodation. In winter when the river is in spate, the Round House looks out across a watery scene as the river comes up to within a few yards of the walls.

From Matrimony Farm, the lane is known as Lower Lane or Jiggy Joggy, perhaps referring to the bumpy ride for those travelling by car to **Charlton All Saints**. The footpath continues through the centre of the village towards Downton. In 1981 a Saxon cemetery containing 43 graves was discovered while the main A338 nearby was being straightened; it is believed that a battle between the Jutes and Ambrosius was fought near here.

The village dates from the medieval period. It was built as a street village on either side of the main road for the tenants of Downton Manor, near the shallows and islands of Charlton Broads, where it is still possible to cross the river to the east bank. From the fourteenth to the eighteenth centuries, the village grew with increasing prosperity and many large farms were built. At the south end of the village we pass Charlton Dairy Farm, one of the few farms that remained after Earl Radnor's enclosure of common land. Today, walking down Lower Lane, the street scene is one of a mixture of new and seventeenth century timber-framed, thatched cottages and a row of nineteenth century Longford estate houses with brick porches.

Leaving the village, the view across the valley to Trafalgar House, set amidst beech trees on the opposite bank of the river is impressive. This house was built in 1733 by John James for Sir Peter Vandeput. It was bought by a grateful nation in 1814 for William Nelson, who was given the title of Earl of Nelson in honour of his brother Horatio. The house was given to the Nelson family in recognition of Horatio's service to his country. The Nelson family subsequently played an important role in the life of Charlton village, funding the building of the church in 1851 and assisting with the funding of the village school, which today has been converted into a private house.

Beyond Charlton the path continues across the water meadows, where there is much evidence of the intricate irrigation system which was used throughout the Avon valley from 1635. It was first developed at Dinton on the River Ebble and is peculiar to the chalk rivers of the South of England. The rain which soaked into the chalk was naturally enriched with minerals and nutrients, and as it re-emerged as small chalk streams in the winter it was warm, and encouraged the early growth of spring grass. This type of irrigation was known in the Avon valley as drowning. Through a system of gates, hatches and sluices, the water was channelled along carriers to the water meadows which were arranged at an angle to the river. The water flowed at a controlled rate along the raised carriers, until it gently overflowed the banks. Only enough water was allowed to flow over the meadows to permeate about an inch into the soil to the roots of the grass. The surface of the meadows was sloped so that the water flowed evenly across them into drains and did not lie in stagnant pools. The drains then carried the surplus water back to the river. The flow of water was controlled by drowners who were responsible for the opening and closing of the sluice gates at pre-arranged watering times.

Along the Ebble, where the river cuts through the chalk downland below Dogdean Farm, the drowning took place in early spring to promote the growth of grass for the lambs which were brought down each day from the downland. It was said that an acre of water meadow could support 400 ewes and their lambs for one day. At night they returned to the ploughland where they were folded and their excrement was used as fertiliser. In April the sheep were removed and the valley was flooded again with the warm alkaline water and a crop of hay could be cut by June. By repeated drowning of the meadows it would be possible to take a second or a third hay crop.

South of Salisbury, the river was enriched with the detritus of the city. Blood from the slaughter houses, animal and human waste of all kinds was washed off the streets during rain storms and winter flooding and brought down to the water meadows by the swollen river. This particularly enriched the meadows around Britford, where this system of irrigation is still in use today. By the early 1800s, with the coming of railways, which enabled the speedy dispersal of dairy products around the country, herds of dairy cattle became more common on these water meadows than sheep.

This system of artificial flooding was increasingly popular through the eighteenth century until the increasing imports of grain, beef and lamb and the use of artificial fertilisers led to the reduction in the numbers of sheep kept on the downs, and early grazing became less important. Eventually the system fell into disrepair. Further south where there were large dairy herds, the system remained in use longer, but it was very labour intensive and eventually uneconomic. The drains became choked with weeds and broken by the cattle and they were finally abandoned. It is still possible to see the remains as far as Ibsley, as the water meadows are criss-crossed with water carriers and crossed by small bridges and sluice gates.

It is often thought that this system of irrigation was introduced by a Dutch engineer held as a prisoner of war at the chapter house in Salisbury. However, this is not the case; the system has been in use since the seventeenth century and the ironwork on some of the hatches, especially near Charlton, was made by Mr Benjamin Dutch at his foundry in Warminster and carry his mark B. Dutch War.

The path towards Downton rejoins the old main road and passes the east face of **New Court Farm**, with its wonderful oak front door.

New Court Farm was first built between 1415 and 1418 as a new manorial centre on the Bishop of Winchester's demesne, and may have been the place

Water meadows with cattle.

where court was held after the removal of Old Court from an island near the Moot in Downton. In 1651 it was sold to Sir Joseph Ashe, a wealthy London merchant. It is some indication of the wealth that was derived from agriculture, and water meadows especially, that Sir Joseph was prepared to invest £11,000 in the acquisition of the farm and a further £2000 to enable his steward, John Snow, to convert the water meadows by introducing the new drowning or floating system of irrigation. It was a period of great population growth and he was soon able to rebuild the farmhouse in a T shape facing the river. Within fifty years he extended it with a west face to form an H. An Act of Parliament in 1664 which enabled the river to be made navigable from Christchurch to Salisbury caused Sir Joseph and other land owners along the valley many problems. In 1686 a canal was constructed across the Longford estate from just above Britford to south of Longford Castle. Sir Joseph assessed that he had to construct 77 small bridges across the carriers to enable men and horses to walk up the river bank alongside the barges. Many of these can still be used today. The level of water in the river was carefully monitored; the farmers could not take out too much at any one time for drowning as a certain depth of water was required not only for the barges but also for the millers to drive their water wheels and for the fishermen. Watering times were carefully controlled and the building of any obstruction across the river was made illegal. It was said in 1794 by Thomas Davies, 'There is, perhaps no part of this Kingdom where the system of watering meadows is so well understood and carried to so great satisfaction as in this district.'

Across the river from New Court Farm is Barford Park Farm or Bereford, all that remains of a large estate bought by a goldsmith banker, Sir Charles Duncombe, in 1690. Sir Charles gained permission to demolish Standlynch Mill and to create a water meadow system on the east bank of the river.

Bereford by Corinna

> This gentle stream, obsequious to command,
> Is taught to overflow the thirsty land,
> and when the moist'ned earth new heat requires,
> Through proper drains immediately retires.
> Hence numerous herds are in those meadows fed,
> Which once nought else but useless rushes bred;
> Hence loads of grass, and never-failing crops,
> With plenteous harvest bless the farmer's hopes.
> At a small distance rise delightful hills,
> Adorn'd with woods and fields, and murm'ring rills.

From New Court Farm it is a pleasant stroll across Catherine Mead, enjoying the view of the roof line of Downton and the church and then along the river bank to Catherine Bridge, or Iron Bridge as it is now known, to the centre of Downton.

To reach the bus stop, turn right at the Iron Bridge and walk west along the Borough, past the White Horse Inn, the original coaching inn serving the road to Charlton, and on to the main A338 Fordingbridge to Salisbury road. Turn right and walk a short way to the north towards Salisbury to the bus stop.

ODSTOCK to DOWNTON
4 MILES

Public Transport
Bus service from:
Salisbury to Woodfalls 44, 43, 45
Ringwood, Bournemouth and Poole to Salisbury, X3
Alternate buses only pass through Odstock to the crossroads in the afternoon
only. Otherwise the bus stop at the Odstock turn off on the A338 is approximately half a mile away

Where to Park
The Yew Tree Inn car park – with permission only. Tel. (01722) 329786
Off road parking on the approach road from the A338 just beyond the school is
approximately 200 yds from the crossroad. From the crossroad, walk past the
Yew Tree Inn and a few yards beyond its car park, turn left to join the Avon
Valley Path.

Where to Stay
Accommodation list from the Tourist Information Office, Fish Row, Salisbury
Tel. (01722) 324956.
The Yew Tree Inn Tel. (01722) 329786
The Warren, 15 High Street, Downton Tel. (01725) 510263
The Kings Arms, High Street, Downton Tel. (01725) 510446

Where to Eat
The Yew Tree Inn, Odstock
The Radnor Arms, Nunton
The Kings Arms, Downton
There are shops to buy picnic food in Downton.

Directions
Continue across the road and up a narrow track between houses to a stile.
Cross the field diagonally right to a field gate, the track runs behind the farm.
Pass through two more gates on either side of a farmyard into a large field.
Cross this field diagonally to the south-east, heading for a clump of trees where
the hedge boundary of the next two fields meets this one. Cross the stile and
follow the left hand field boundary to a gate. Continue to a tarmac lane. After
approximately 200 yds where the lane bends to the left the Avon Valley
Footpath continues straight ahead on an unsurfaced track.

Follow the track gradually uphill for about $1/2$ mile to the field and continue
straight ahead (south). Cross a stile, passing under the power line. Follow the
field boundary to the stile in the far corner. After this stile immediately turn left

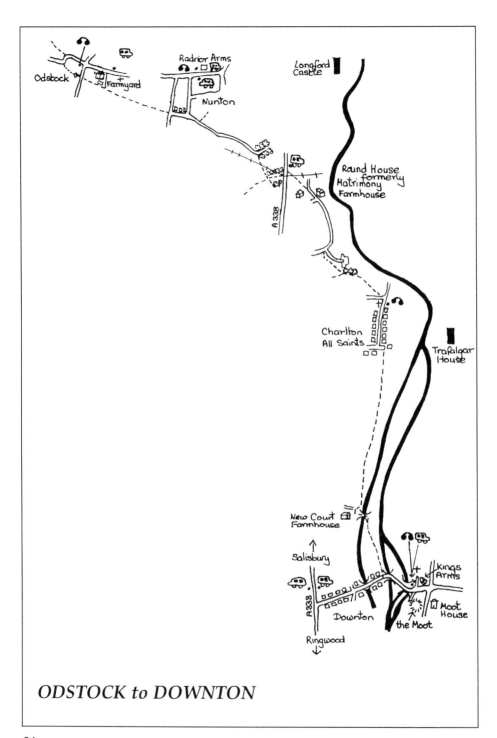

Odstock

Farmyard

Radnor Arms

Nunton

Longford Castle

A 338

Round House formerly Matrimony Farmhouse

Charlton All Saints

Trafalgar House

New Court Farmhouse

Salisbury

A 338

Downton

Ringwood

Kings Arms

Moot House

the Moot

ODSTOCK to DOWNTON

to proceed down hill following the field boundary with a hedge on the left, to a small hunting gate beside the pylon to the main Salisbury-Ringwood Road.

Cross the A338 (signposted to Ringwood) with care to a clearly marked Avon Valley Footpath signpost. A pair of stiles leads into the field. Cross diagonally towards a gate in the far right-hand corner of the field, passing under the power lines. Pass through the gate, turn right onto a lane and proceed to Matrimony Farm. Where the road bends to the right, bear left and cross a stile beside a metal farm gate. Walk beside the farm track to a stile.

Cross the next field diagonally right to a third stile in the opposite right hand corner. Follow the hedge to a stile onto a track signed Charlton All Saints $^3/_4$ mile. Turn right onto this farm track for 100 yards to a kissing gate. Proceed on the permissive route to stile leading into a lane. Turn left onto the lane and follow it to Charlton All Saints church.

At the T junction by the church, turn right onto Lower Road and follow it through the village. At the end of the village where the road bends to the right, turn left onto a track. After 50 yards, turn right over a stile and walk over several fields towards Downton. At the entrance to New Court Farm, turn left over the farm bridge and follow the gravel track beside the water course. After 100 yards cross a wooden footbridge and follow the path across the water meadows to the banks of the Avon and so to Downton. For those wishing to finish the walk here, turn left and walk through the village to the traffic lights on the main A338; the X3 bus stop for Salisbury or Bournemouth is a few yards to the right.

Section 3
DOWNTON

Downton, which once the Royal presence shar'd
To Windsor Castle should be still compared.

Downton is the oldest town on the route. As the path passes through the town, it takes you back through the centuries. Standing on the bridge and looking down into the clear River Avon you may be lucky enough to see a trout or two lurking there, nearly camouflaged against the river bed; a reminder of the reason Downton came into existence.

It was here that several roads converged and ancient man was able to ford the river. Roads such as Wick Lane, which led west to Cranborne and Poole and north to Wilton Way, Shaston Drove and Salt Lane, which led north-east over Pepperbox Hill to Winchester, transporting salt which had been brought upriver by boat from the coast, and nearby Cloven Way, which led south-east to Southampton. During the twelfth century a medieval wooden bridge was built over the ford; it became a meeting place where people came to talk and barter their wares. So Downton became a market town not by charter, but by prescription. In 1208 Bishop Peter des Roches, lord of the manor of Downton and

*Iron Bridge, Downton showing thatched home and
workshop of basket maker Mr Eastman.*

Bishop of Winchester, appreciating the commercial potential of the town and perhaps vying with Salisbury, planned an extension to the existing village to create a borough planned on a grid system. The sites were offered with the additional incentive of a free burgage tenure, which gave each property owner a voting right. The bishop's paramount interest was in the financial returns from the market. The market area stretched from the west bank across the Bishop's Meadows to the Headlands, being the beginning of the arable land. The word headland means the point at the end of the field where the plough turns. This point is now marked by the traffic lights on the A338. The market was one of the largest in the country planned at that time and equals in size that of Wenceslas Square in Prague, which with many others all over Britain and Europe was being developed at the time. Only those proposed by kings, bishops and wealthy land owners were planned; others grew at random as land was sold off. The market at Downton was officially recognised in 1289 as a cattle and horse market. It was held every Thursday until 1792, when they could no longer compete with Salisbury. There were also two fairs, one held on 2 October, and the other, the Cuckoo Fair, on 23 April. Today there is one fair held on May Day weekend. In 1735 the bridge was rebuilt as a three-arched stone bridge and extended in 1820 with iron balustrading, which explains why today it is called the Iron Bridge.

The first house to the west on the north side of the road, was once the home and workshop of Mr Eastman, who was the last basket maker in Downton. This was once a thriving industry in the Avon Valley, which today has all but died out. The Eastman family had been working from this house since 1765, cutting willows from the osier beds and reeds and weaving them into baskets. The same skills were needed in the manufacture of eel traps and lobster pots, although these were usually made of hazel wands.

Turn left from the bridge and you will find the road crosses an island, thence past some nineteenth-century houses and over Tannery Bridge to the old town on the rising ground of the east bank.

There has been a tannery in Downton since 1606, utilising the site's constant supply of water, oak bark from the New Forest and hides from the dairy herds kept on the water meadows. The present building dates from 1919, and Downton Tanning Company processes 200 hides a day. The prepared hides are used in the manufacture of shoes and riding equipment, the best quality being used for the production of ballet shoes. In 1859 there were seven shoemaking businesses in Downton, but the last one closed in 1923.

Opposite the tannery are the two mills which remain out of the original seven owned by the bishops of Winchester in 1086. Both would have been corn mills in Saxon times. The mill to the west had been converted into a paper mill by 1781, when the paper was used in the production of bank notes. The easterly mill beside the Waterside was bought by the owners of the tannery, and in 1929 it was converted to generate electricity for their own use. Eventually it was run by the Downton Electric Light Company, which was taken over by the Central Electricity Generating Board in 1948. It was closed in 1973.

Beyond the mill is the Waterside, once called Watershoot Lane, a short cul-de-sac terminating at the mill foot and overlooked by an attractive row of nineteenth-century cottages built in the Elizabethan style. Looking south across the mill foot, it is possible to see an island where it is believed the bishops built themselves a residence known as Old Court, to which King John came from the royal palace at Clarendon to enjoy the local hunting. It is known that he visited here on his way to Wareham in 1215, shortly after signing the Magna Carta.

The footpath continues along the High Street past Tannery House to the square. On the left is Church Hatch, leading to **St Laurence's Church**.

The origins of this church date back to Birinus, who was considered the Apostle of Wessex, as he brought Christianity to the region from Italy in the early seventh century. He became the first bishop of the Saxons. Having begun a mission in Oxford, his see was moved to Winchester, and thus he consecrated the first church at Downton in 638 AD. The present church has a Norman nave but principally dates from the thirteenth century and is of flint and stone construction. The church was dedicated in 1147 and in 1382 it was appropriated by William Wykeham, then Bishop of Winchester. He used the tithes which the church collected to maintain 70 scholars in a college to be founded in Winchester. This school is now the well known Winchester College.

Today the church is kept locked, but there are several things of interest which can be seen from outside. Look out for the mass dial marked on the church wall. This operated like a sundial, but the lines marked on the stone were designed to indicate the time of mass rather than the time of day. On the south side of the chancel wall is a low leper window, and a careful look at the end wall of the south transept will reveal the outline of a large wide door. This is all that remains to confirm that the town's fire engine was housed in the church in the early part of the nineteenth century. In 1791 the Earl of Radnor ordered that the tower should be doubled in height so that he could see it from his estate, but by 1860 it had become so unstable that it was reduced to its present height.

Beyond the church through a private door in the wall and just visible from the graveyard, is Parsonage Manor House. During the fifteenth century the lands held by the Bishop of Winchester were divided between two manors: the Bishop's Manor which in the nineteenth century became the property of the Earl of Radnor, and Parsonage Manor, which was given to Winchester College. The manor house is believed to be the oldest continuously inhabited house in the south of England, possibly dating from AD 850, the land having been given to the church in AD 826 by Egbert, King of the West Saxons. The wing furthest from the church was built as a parsonage in the fourteenth century.

In 1576 Queen Elizabeth I applied to Winchester College for permission to rent the house, with the ulterior motive of giving it to Thomas Wilkes, who had been clerk to the Privy Council. She was refused at first, but after pressure was brought to bear the college relented. The house was later sold to Sir Walter Raleigh's mother and brother, Carew Raleigh, who served as MP for Downton. The family owned the house for approximately a hundred years during which time Sir Walter Raleigh owned Sherborne Castle.

At some time when the Raleigh family owned the house, perhaps when Sir Walter was executed in 1618, a portrait of him painted in 1588 was hidden behind the oak panelling. It was found about two hundred and fifty years later by a farmer who, in the late nineteenth century, like many other farmers at the time, was facing bankruptcy. He gave the picture to a Salisbury land-agent, Humberts, against a bad debt, and subsequently, in 1857, it became the first purchase of the National Portrait Gallery for £105, and is now the best known portrait of Sir Walter Raleigh.

Returning to the square, you pass an old malt house on the right hand side; this is one of three which existed in Downton in 1810, and which were still in use into the twentieth century. It was here that barley used in the production of beer would be malted. The process involved soaking the barley and allowing it to begin germination before drying it in a kiln.

Turn left at the fourteenth-century King's Arms inn on the corner and follow the road up the hill past the Warren on the left. It is believed that this was once an ecclesiastical residence, as the lawns stretch down to the church. It also has a fine panelled bedroom which it is believed was brought here after the demolition of Old Court. From the name, it is believed that the bishop's warrener

Sir Walter Raleigh.
Courtesy of the National Portrait
Gallery, London.

may have lived here or that his warren may have been in the grounds, for in medieval times rabbits were rare and carefully nurtured animals, kept in artificial warrens and protected from the cold in the winter.

Opposite the Downton Inn, turn right into Moot Lane. On the left is Moot House, a fine house with a pair of wonderful iron gates. The house is a restoration of the previous house built in 1650 which was gutted by fire in 1926.

Opposite are eighteenth-century landscaped gardens, with a Greek temple and amphitheatre where occasional concerts and plays are still performed. At the turn of the century, three-day fêtes were held here, attended by about 3000 people. There were fireworks displays, dancing and torchlight processions, as well as theatrical performances. They were so popular that special trains were laid on from Salisbury and Bournemouth to the railway station which existed a short walk from the gardens at that time.

The conical man-made mound in the centre of the gardens – now called **the Moot** – was originally a Bronze Age fortification. As a dun or dune, it gave its name to the settlement of Dunton, as it was called in the *Anglo-Saxon Chronicle*. The Saxons subsequently used it as an open air meeting place – a moot. The hillocks on either side were named the Hill of Judgement and Hill of Execution, where it is recorded that criminals were executed.

Looking out from the Moot there is a panoramic view across the Avon Valley, and it is possible to pick out nearly all the nearby sites inhabited by the ancient British. To the south-west are Breamore Woods, and just to their west are the Mizmaze and Witsbury Castle ditches. Due west is Gallows Hill and to the north-west is Clearbury Rings, a distinct isolated hill fortification overgrown with beech trees and a clump of Scots pine. Due north it is possible to see Figsbury Ring and to the north-east is Pepperbox Hill.

It is known that the Saxons, led by Cerdic, their Jutish leader, came up Southampton Water and landed near Totton. They then moved west across the New Forest along what would be known as the Cloven Way until they reached the east bank of the River Avon. The river halted their advance until a great battle was fought on the south of Downton at Charford or 'Cerdic's Ford', and there they defeated the Romano British and were able to advance across the river to Clearbury and beyond. Saeroyrg, otherwise known as Old Sarum, was finally captured by Cerdic's son, Cynric, in AD 552 .

After their conversion to Christianity, the Saxons gave their Downton stronghold to the Bishop of Winchester, who presided over the council meetings of the hundred moot with the local thanes.

Downton's political influence was to continue until 1832, when the Reform Bill was passed. Since 1395 Downton had returned two Members to Parliament. This continued even after the town's importance as a market and ecclesiastical centre had waned. During the eighteenth century Downton had been very important as a burgage borough; this meant that every property owner had the right to vote. Each house still has its voting number displayed on the front. The system, however, could be abused. Through bribery or by owning numerous properties, wealthy landowners were able to control (or pocket) the votes to ensure their return to Parliament. It was therefore not a coincidence that the two MPs who represented Downton were the owners of the two manors, Parsonage Manor and Bishop's Manor. By 1832 public opinion against these pocket boroughs, particularly from the unenfranchised new industrial conurbations, led to the reform of the electoral system. It is said that when the Bill was passed there was great rejoicing in the streets of Salisbury, the bells were rung, the city was illuminated and 2600 people dined in the Market Place.

Continuing along Moot Lane past Moor Farm the path turns left just beyond

View across Dowton from the Moot.

the recently converted barn. Further along Moot Lane and to the right in Castle Meadows is a housing estate, and it is worth pondering a moment that this estate is built upon the oldest part of Downton. Beneath the houses lie the remains of the seasonal camp of the Mesolithic people. An excavation in 1956 revealed the stake holes and flint blades of the only known settlement in Wiltshire, dating back to the fourth century BC. These people were the early nomadic hunter gatherers who preceded the Neolithic settlers, whom we know by their long barrows and cursus, and the Bronze Age people who built the hilltop forts and defended enclosures such as **Clearbury**. Also found during the excavations were the remains of a third century Roman farmstead which was probably deserted when the Saxons arrived.

Continue up the hill to the top of the ridge. This is a fine place to stop a while and look back at the view over Downton and beyond to the spire of Salisbury Cathedral. The view of Clearbury is quite spectacular. It is easy to see how Gough described it in his *Camden Britannica* in 1789 as 'a very great single camp called Clerebury, with a beacon in it'.

Section 4
DOWNTON TO FORDINGBRIDGE
7 MILES

Bereford by Corinna

When with the dawn my joyful eyes decried
Sarum's high spire, the wanderers certain guide,
Whose lofty summit seems to touch the sky
to the delighted but deluded eye.
The well-known object, pleasing to my view,
Reviv'd my peace, and did my hopes renew.

Hence looking outwards, the surveying eye
A large and various prospect doth descry:
Towns, churches, mountains, pleasant fields, and woods,
Enamel'd meadows, and transparent floods,
Below the kine, the fleecy sheep above,
In numerous flocks about their pasture rove.
Hills gently rising terminate the site,
And close the landscape with complete delight.

From the top of the ridge above Downton, turn right and the footpath heads south towards Hale. The route along the edge of the ridge passes by some ancient woodland and hedges with some mature ash, oak, hazel and elder. Dr Max Hooper investigated the age of hedges and discovered that by counting the number of species present in a 30 yard stretch, it was possible to date the hedge at approximately one hundred years for each different species. This does not include ramblers such as bramble or honeysuckle. Other indications of ancient woodland and hedgerows are the presence of flowers such as primroses, bluebells, celandines, wood anenomes and dog mercury. They are also found growing under old hedges which were created by leaving a strip of woodland whilst otherwise clearing the trees for agriculture.

This is a very pretty section of the walk in the spring, as the woods are carpeted with bluebells, and primroses grow on banks alongside the roads.

The path passes Park Ashes Copse on the right, with its stand of tall Douglas fir; after crossing a stile in the valley bottom it passes Dark Copse to the left, this is mainly a hazel copse. Lodge Farm can be seen nestling in the valley across the fields to the west.

Just beyond the next stile the path crosses Lodge Drove, a green way whose banks are covered with primroses, bluebells, anemomes and aconites beneath holly, ash and pine. It is probable that this drove road from Woodfalls to Lodge Farm was the northern arm of the Saxon route, the Cloven Way, which crossed here.

Before reaching the Hatchet Green road, the path passes through the picturesque farmyard of Hatchet Gate Farm, an early cob and thatch farmhouse.

Before following the Avon Valley Path along the road to the right, take a look around **Hatchet Green** on the left. The green, which covers a total area of 13 acres, is bounded to the east by a Bronze Age barrow called Windmill Ball; in a seventeenth-century description it is referred to as Churl's Hill, a churl being a free peasant dependent on the lord of the manor, but living on the edge of his land. To the south is the village school, and to the west is a thatched cottage, once a Dame School, which in the eighteenth and nineteenth centuries was the forerunner of the modern nursery school. The green is used both as the school playground and on summer Saturday afternoons as the village cricket pitch.

It is believed that the road through Hatchet Green follows the route of the southern arm of the old Saxon road, the 'Cloven Way'. This route led past the round barrow across the Green and west back down the road towards Hale House. The road passes on the left Hatchet Lodge, a wonderful example of a baroque gate house at the start of the lime tree avenue planted in 1715 by Thomas Archer. This avenue of mature trees runs parallel with the road as far as Hale House. There are some wonderful views from the road across the Avon

Hale House.

Valley to Breamore Woods and Gallows Hill as the road drops downhill between high banks to Home Farm. From here it is believed that the Saxon path continued down through a hollow way and then across the river to South Charford Farm and up to Gallows Hill. Today the path leads down beside the lime trees to **Hale House** and the church of St Mary of Hale.

A house on this site dates back to the Norman Conquest when Ulviet, the King's huntsman, lived there. It may even be an older site, as Hale is a Celtic word meaning a corner or nook. By the fourteenth century a house on this site was owned by the Penruddock family. It was Colonel Penruddock who incriminated Dame Alicia Lisle of Moyles Court during the Monmouth Rebellion and caused her to be executed at Winchester in 1685.

Hale Park was bought in 1715 by Thomas Archer, one of the country's four most famous English baroque architects; in fact the only one of the four to study in Italy, the other three being Sir Christopher Wren, Vanburgh and Hawksmoor. Apart from rebuilding Hale House and the church of **St Mary of Hale**, he also designed Heythrop Hall, St John's Church, Westminster, the north wing of Chatsworth House and in 1705 the church of St Philip, Birmingham, now the cathedral. He is buried in the church of St Mary of Hale, where there are fine memorials by Peer Scheemaker and Richard Westmacott, who both produced memorials for the church of St Laurence at Downton.

The path leads down through Church Copse, a knoll encircled with conifer yews which have grown to a great height. These trees are common in the county and are known as the Hampshire weed. Opposite the bottom of the path there is a footbridge and, when dry, it is possible to cross the river and walk to the Saxon church and village of Breamore approximately two miles away, where it is well worth visiting Breamore House and Countryside Museum.

From the bottom of the path, turn left (south) and follow the road a short distance until the path turns left to the village of **Woodgreen**. This was once described as 'a village in a mantle of white' when the merry trees for which it was famous were in blossom. Merry trees are a form of wild cherry, whose black fruit was made into a wonderful jam. These trees have nearly all gone, but scenes depicting fruit picking and other village activities can be seen in the village hall near the shop and the Horse and Groom pub in the centre of the village. In 1932, when Vaughan Nash, private secretary to Lord Asquith, lived in the village, he invited his friend Sir William Rothenstein to stay. Sir William was the principal of a London art college and had a particular interest in reviving the ancient technique of mural painting; it was about the time that Rex Whistler painted the walls of the tea rooms at the Tate Gallery in London. Rothenstein secured a grant of £100 from the Carnegie Trust, which enabled him to engage two of his students, who under his leadership undertook to paint all the walls of the hall to test out various techniques. It took eighteen months to complete, in which time the students, R.W. Baker and E.P. Payne, known as the Mansard Group, painted no fewer than 50 portraits of local residents in murals depicting village life, scenes such as Sunday School, Morris Dancing, the Cricket Club, and various rural activities. The mural recently featured in a BBC documentary entitled 'The village on the wall' and is well worth a detour. Do telephone first for the key, to Mrs Windel (caretaker) on (01725) 512529 or Mrs Sales on (01725) 512288.

Woodgreen, like so many New Forest settlements having no lord of the manor, vicar or other clear authority, attracted free thinkers and vagrants who settled in the Forest clearing. They came especially during periods of political unrest such as the Peasants Revolt, the Black Death, the Dissolution of the Monasteries and the Civil War, or when they were experiencing religious persecution or because of unwanted pregnancies. They became squatters on the land, and provided they were able to enclose about half an acre of land and erect a dwelling with a hearth and chimney for a fire before being challenged, they were able to establish themselves as smallholders. These homesteads were entitled to Forest Rights, the Right of Turbary – to cut turf for fuel – the Right of Pasture – to turn cattle and ponies out onto the forest to graze – and the Right of Pannage – to turn a pig out onto the forest in the late autumn to eat the acorns. Other rights included the right to cut bracken for bedding and the right to dig clay. These enabled the squatters to become self-sufficient and to keep two cows, a pig and a pony.

In 1670 a Royal Commission was set up to survey all the Forest properties and to make sure that further squatters could not set up home. However, the officials received such poor pay that they were open to bribery. It was after this time that the original squatters' cottages were upgraded. The cob and thatch dwellings in the village today, especially along Brook Lane, date from this time. The small settlement gradually grew into a community and increased in size. By 1885, after the arrival of the railway, many visitors came from Salisbury, Poole and Bournemouth to take walking tours in the New Forest. One of the nearest stations with access to the Forest was Breamore, and commoners from Woodgreen were hired as guides for these expeditions. Expansion was rapid at this time, as 'desirable residences' were built for people seeking privacy, hunting and fishing.

From Woodgreen, follow the road around the ancient earthworks of **Castle Hill**, from where there are some magnificent views across the Avon Valley. Looking north-west, it is possible to see Breamore House and the mill below Woodgreen. It is the scene reproduced in the mural painting of the poachers in the village hall. At Folds Farm, the path turns west across the water meadows to the suspension bridge at Burgate Manor Farm. This bridge was built in 1950 by Hampshire County Council to replace the original wooden cattle bridge destroyed by a tank during the Second World War. The new bridge was built of metal at a cost of £1000, as wood was in short supply after the war. It is a most elegant bridge in a tranquil setting, where Kingfishers are a common sight flying low over the water. The path continues past the seventeenth-century Burgate Manor Farmhouse to the main Fordingbridge to Salisbury road. This is a medieval road connecting Fordingbridge, **Burgate** and Breamore. In 1860 there were six stage coaches a week travelling to Salisbury, visiting such coaching inns as the Red Lion and the Black Horse in Salisbury. Rouse's Coaches ran tours from Cross Keys in Salisbury to Fordingbridge and back in the day. The Tudor Rose, which stands invitingly beside the main road, has only been a pub in recent years, having been converted from a pair of farm cottages.

Heading west from the A338, the path crosses the route of the disused Poole to Salisbury railway line, which was opened on 20 December 1866, with four trains running to Poole each day, stopping at Downton, Breamore,

View from Castle Hill across the Avon Valley.

Fordingbridge and Alderholt. A wide detour was necessary round Somerley Park, as Lord Normanton, who owned the land south of Harbridge, refused to allow the line to cross his estate. The use of the line declined over the next hundred years, until in 1964 it fell under Beeching's axe and was closed. On the left of the path can still be seen the gate keeper's cottage, now painted white, standing beside the remains of the concrete fence posts, the gate having long since gone. As the path follows the boundary of the Burgate School, built in 1957, it passes a pillbox, an apt reminder of the war when German bomber planes followed the river up the valley en route to the Midlands. At least 500 bombs were dropped in the area, but miraculously only one house was damaged.

The path joins the Whitsbury Road, another medieval route linking Fordingbridge to Breamore, and enters the town of Fordingbridge, referred to by Trollope as Silverbridge.

At the junction with Salisbury Street is the Old Manor Court House for the Manor of Burgate, built in 1600.

DOWNTON to FORDINGBRIDGE
7 MILES

Public Transport
Bus service from:
Salisbury to Bournemouth X3, alight at The Bull
Woodfalls to Salisbury 44, 43
Hale to Fordingbridge and Ringwood 39
Salisbury to Swanage, Sundays in summer only, X81
From the bus stop on the A338, walk to the traffic lights and turn left in The
Borough. Walk along The Borough to the second bridge – the Iron Bridge – over
the river.

Where to Park
Anywhere beside the road and walk to the Iron Bridge.

Where to Stay
Accommodation list from the Tourist Information Office, Fish Row, Salisbury
Tel. (01722) 334956.
The Kings Arms, High Street, Downton Tel. (01725) 510446
Sandy Balls Estate Holiday Centre, Fordingbridge Tel. (01425) 653042

Where to Eat
The Kings Arms, Downton
There are shops to buy picnic food in Downton.
Horse and Groom public house, Woodgreen
Ivy Cottage Tea Rooms, Burgate

Places to Visit
The Moot, Moot Lane, Downton
St Lawrence Church, Downton
Church of St Mary of Hale
Breamore House
The Village Hall, Woodgreen

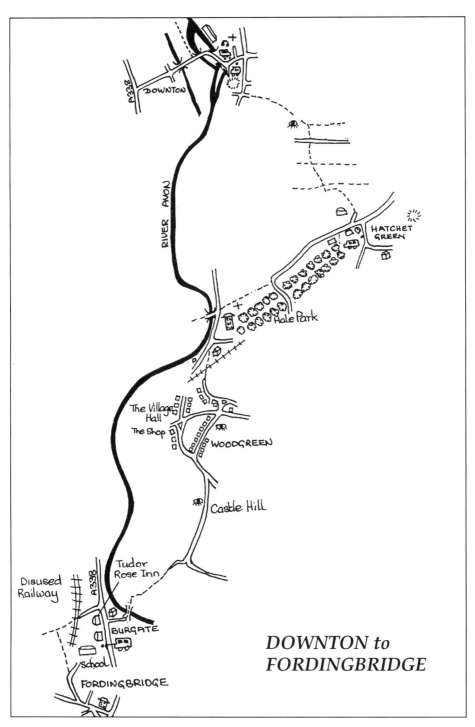

DOWNTON to
FORDINGBRIDGE

Directions

The Avon Valley Path turns left over the river bridge and passes the tannery on the left. Continue uphill and turn right into Moot Lane. Just beyond Moot Farm, turn left onto a track between the barn and the housing estate. This leads to a stile and a path that runs along the right side of the field beneath the power lines. Cross a stile. Follow the power lines through open fields. Halfway up, after about $^1/_4$ mile, cross the stile on the right and cut the corner of this field uphill to cross a further stile onto a farm track.

Turn right and follow the farm track south to its junction with Drove Road. Cross this road to a stile in the hedge. The path follows the right hand boundary of the field and down a steep valley to a stile in the valley bottom. Continue up the hill beside a hazel coppice on the left to a stile.

Cross an old sunken drove road which leads from Redlynch to Lodge Farm. Ignore the stile and gate on the left and continue straight on through the wooded area with a wire fence on the right, uphill to the corner of the field. Follow the fence round to the left until you encounter a stile with Hampshire written on it; follow the direction indicated and proceed diagonally left across a field to the second yellow marker at the corner of the copse. Turn right over the stile and follow the path downhill alongside the copse, over the stile and footbridge and re-enter the wood via the stile and footbridge at the valley bottom. Continue uphill through woodland, cross another stile and carry on uphill to a small farm. Enter the farmyard with a thatched cottage and follow the farm track which leads eventually to a gate onto a tarmac lane. If you have time turn left to see Hale Green.

The Avon Valley Path turns right (west-south-west) at this point. Follow the road for about $^1/_2$ mile until reaching a sharp left hand bend. Continue round the bend and turn right onto a signposted footpath beside the avenue of trees which leads to the church of St Mary of Hale, passing Hale House on the left.

Descend the tarmac path to the road. Turn left and follow the road beside the river for a $^1/_4$ mile towards Woodgreen. At the T junction, turn right and almost immediately turn left to enter a drive to Hale Rectory. Cross a stile after the cattle grid and follow a field-edge path alongside the field boundary, crossing three stiles to a gravel track. Continue uphill through the outskirts of the village along the gravel track, bearing right at the fork at the top until the track emerges opposite the Common.

Cross the tarmac road and follow the narrow lane opposite south beside the Green. Continue along the lane downhill, crossing a stream to a T junction. By turning right here it is possible to reach the village centre where there is a shop, a pub and the Grade II listed village hall. Turn left and continue on the road leading uphill. After 250 yards, turn first right near a Woodgreen sign onto a narrow road leading to Castle Hill. Follow this road for $^3/_4$ mile until it runs downhill. At the bottom of the hill just beyond a drive to a house where a stream crosses under the road turn right and follow the stream to a stile at Folds

Farm. There is no sign on the road, do not miss the turning. Cross the stile by the farm entrance gate. Follow the gravel track and at the farmyard continue straight ahead with the farmyard on the right and pass through a metal gate. Ignoring the first and second footpath signs to the left, continue over a low rise and walk west downhill to the water meadows. The path continues in the same direction via a series of concrete bridges for $^1/_2$ mile before turning left to reach a white suspension bridge. Turn right after the suspension bridge, go through the farmyard and walk to the end of the drive past the farmhouse.

After emerging onto the A338 opposite the Hourglass Restaurant, turn right for about 50 yds, heading back towards Salisbury. Pass the Tudor Rose Inn on the left and just beyond the inn car park, turn left to enter a gravel track to Burgate Farm and Keepers Gate. Continue straight ahead down a long farm track for 400 yds behind Burgate school. At an old grass junction where three fields meet turn left on a grass track leading to Fordingbridge. The path merges with Penny's Lane, which should be followed straight ahead to a T junction. Turn left into Whitsbury Road. At the junction with Green Lane bear left and follow the road to the T junction with the main road through Fordingbridge. Turn right past the Post Office to the mini-roundabout with Lloyds Bank on the corner. Turn right into the High Street and continue for about 200 yds before taking the left hand fork into Provost Street. Cross the river and continue to the left into Church Street.

Section 5
FORDINGBRIDGE TO IBSLEY
4 MILES

'T'is said of mortals in this place
That we are a very funny race
And one of our peculiar ways
We only get up alternate days

No more we hear that worn out phrase
about the way we used to laze
We get up regular every day
And think it much the nicest way

No one seems to know the origin of this little ditty, but it is how the people of **Fordingbridge** were described at the beginning of this century. I doubt that it would have been an apt description during the Middle Ages, when the town, at that time called Forde, grew up round the river crossing on the boundary between two royal chases, the New Forest to the east and Cranborne Chase to the west.

Although the town was essentially medieval, the site used as a river crossing dates from at least the Roman period. Pottery from the local Roman potteries at Gorley, Sloden and Godshill supplied not only the domestic pots for the country estate at Rockbourne but also those of Woodyates, Old Sarum and beyond. In 1268, during the reign of Henry III, the original wooden toll bridge was maintained by the chapel of St John on the east bank of the river. It was similar to the chapel beside Harnham Bridge in Salisbury and is believed to have been inhabited by a hermit who collected tolls, acted as a guide to the New Forest and arranged the bridge repairs as required. By 1313 the chapel, now the site of St John's Farm at Horseport, may have been an hospitium for wayfarers. The present bridge with its seven arches was built of iron sandstone from Alderholt in 1362.

There is a good view of the bridge from the riverside garden of the George Inn, where there was a special room known as the Watch Room from which until 1840 a bailiff kept watch over the bridge during the Fence Months. Every year around midsummer, the lord of the manor was obliged to have the bridge guarded and to arrest anyone caught crossing with venison. Special grappling hooks were used to anchor a wagon to the iron railings of the bridge until it had been searched and allowed to continue on its way. Isaac Walton, in his book *The Compleat Angler*, tells us that Fence Months also applied to fishing, 'they be principally three, namely March, April and May; for these be the usual months that

Salmon come out of the sea to spawn in most fresh rivers,' and salmon certainly came up river as far as Fordingbridge; some as large as 40 pounds were caught, although there are few today. It used to be a common sight to see salmon swimming upstream to spawn in the drainage channels across the water meadows, and the drowners received a bonus for any stranded fish they helped to return to the main river. Today the river is famous for its coarse fishing and its trout, although there has been a steady decline since 1975 due partly to pollution from the trout farms up river. Eels are also caught in great numbers; it was said that on a thundery night it was possible to catch between 400 and 600 pounds of eels, which were generally sent to the London markets.

A peculiarity of the river here is that due to underground springs and streams from the chalkland rising beneath the river bed, the river freezes from the bottom upwards. On a cold winter's day, standing on the bridge, it is possible to see bubbles of ice floating to the surface. It is one of only five rivers in the world to behave in this manner.

Looking across the river from the George there is a good view of the recreation ground, where a statue of Augustus John by Ivor Roberts-Jones stands almost hidden by a hedge. He was an artist of international repute but disliked locally on account of his Bohemian lifestyle. He lived for many hears at Fryern Court, Upper Burgate, and died in 1961. During his years at Fordingbridge he painted many portraits, of which his portrait of W.B. Yeats hangs in the Tate Gallery and that of Dylan Thomas can be seen at the National Gallery of Wales in Cardiff. Apart from portraits he painted female nudes, which outraged the Fordingbridge folk. The local New Forest gypsies hailed him as their champion 'King of the Gypsies'. It was at this time that new laws were being introduced which would change the gypsies' way of life. For generations they had been allowed to roam at will across the forest, camping wherever they chose. Although Augustus John was able to persuade the local council to support the gypsies, laws were finally passed outlawing them from living in the Forest.

Most of the buildings to the west of the bridge date from 1702 following a disastrous series of fires destroyed much of the town, which was mainly thatch at the time. The destruction was so great that collections were taken at churches throughout the land 'for the relief of the people of Fordingbridge.'

The road to Church Square from the High Street leads across the Sweatford and Ashford Waters, which both join the Avon at this point. Looking downstream to the left at Knowles Bridge are the Town Mills, now a private house. Fordingbridge was renowned in the eighteenth century for its textile industry. Flax was grown across the river at Stuckton in what are still called Flaxfields, and was processed at East Mills into ticking for mattresses and pillow covers. In 1790 there were 500 looms in the town making cloth. Canvas was also made and sent across the New Forest to Bucklers Hard, where it was used to make sails.

On the left, just before Church Square, is a small industrial development owned by the Shering family. This houses a most interesting private museum which is open by appointment only. A narrow passage beyond the museum is called the Hank – so called after a measurement of flax – which leads into an area known as Great Whitening Yard, where the cloth was originally bleached. This in turn leads to the Riverside Gardens, where there was a rowing and sailing club. It was here that from 1879 until the First World War and for a short while afterwards regattas were held on the river. These were so popular that they attracted people from as far away as London and trains were laid on to bring people to the station at Fordingbridge. They became known as Hampshire's Regattas. It was a very festive occasion, with hundreds of people enjoying the water sports from the illuminated river bank, and no doubt business was brisk at the Black Boy public house in Church Square. This pub, now a pair of cottages, was frequented by the calico printers, dyers and tick makers. Once it was the scene of the capture of the infamous Dorset smuggler, Captain Diamond, otherwise known as the Smuggler King.

In 1747 the preventive men of Poole captured Diamond's boat, *The Three Brothers* and confiscated its cargo, taking the captain and some of his men prisoner in the Custom House in Poole along with the cargo. During the night a raid was mounted on the Custom House to recover the cargo and to release the Captain and Lieutenant Bailey, who escaped on horseback to Fordingbridge, where they shared out the bounty at the George Inn. A battle then followed between the smugglers and the preventive men in Bridge Street, and Captain Diamond and some followers escaped to Whitsbury. Following a proclamation granting a free pardon to any informer, David Smith came forward and gave information leading to Captain Diamond's arrest at the Black Boy. He and his men were hanged at Breamore, Sandleheath, Gorley and Gallows Hill. Later David Smith was ambushed at Telegraph Hill on the Forest nearby. His tongue was cut out and he was beaten and hanged, possibly in Dead Man's Hollow between Telegraph Hill and Godshill.

Overlooking Church Square is the church of **St Mary**. Although built on the site of an original Saxon church, it is principally a thirteenth-century Early English church with an unusual fifteenth-century tower built in the middle. The church was a most important building and, like the bridge, was built of iron sandstone from Alderholt. Inside, the north chapel has a very fine hammer-beam roof of carved chestnut wood. The seven hundred-year-old font was found buried in the Vicarage garden in 1902. Outside in an east bay on the north wall of the church, overlooking the graveyard and close by the Avon Valley Footpath, is set a rectangular stone. There are grooves running down the face of the stone where countless generations of townspeople have scraped at the surface to remove stone dust for its healing powers. It is claimed to be a miracle stone; powder from it was thought to cure all manner of ailments. The path continues south across the water meadows. To the east across the river lies Bicton Mill and Trout Farm. The Avon Valley Path leads to **Harbridge**, a small hamlet of predominantly thatched cottages, which became part of the Somerley

Church of St Mary, Fordingbridge.

estate in 1810. Looking east across the fields, the tower of Harbridge church rises up above the hedgerows. Dating from the fifteenth century, the church was remodelled and the tower raised in 1838 to mark the accession of Queen Victoria. The church also serves the community of **Turmer**, where the village school was built overlooking the duck pond and village green. Although the school has recently been converted into a private dwelling, most of the village has escaped modernisation, as have the farming methods used by Mr Sampson, the local farmer. In the 1950s he continued to farm in the traditional way when most farmers in the country were replacing their farm horses with new tractors. He and his son Robert still breed and work their heavy horses, some of which can be seen grazing or working in the fields around Turmer. They are a French breed known as Percheron, smaller and more compact than shire horses and of a placid temperament. They were first introduced from America during the First World War to pull gun carriages, as they would remain calm under artillery fire. For the same reason they made excellent farm horses and continued to be used as such after the war. The path passes close to Turmer Farm, and often the sound of blacksmithing can be heard coming from the old Victorian barn where Mr Robert Sampson still makes his own horseshoes.

At the end of the drive opposite the duck pond there is a drinking fountain. The sweet water is piped here from the hillside springs, because the water that naturally rises from the valley floor is full of ochre and is virtually undrinkable.

Ibsley Bridge.

Ochre results from the breakdown of iron which naturally occurs in the local water.

Walking from the village of Turmer towards the water meadows it is often possible to see some round ricks in the corner of the field nearest the church. These are made of wheat straw cut on the farm and thatched with sedge spears cut from the river bank in the traditional manner. Local thatchers are supplied with their raw materials from these.

The gravel road leading to the water meadows crosses the so-called Coach Road used by earlier generations of the Normanton family to drive their coach and horses to Harbridge church before the bridge was built across to Ellingham Church. A small footbridge leads into the water meadows, which are an SSSI conservation area maintained without the use of fertilisers and pesticides. As a result, it is a mecca for naturalists. Flowers grow in profusion. In the spring the fields are golden with marsh marigolds and yellow iris, and in the summer white with meadow sweet. The path leads to the edge of the river and follows it upstream for a short way to **Ibsley** Bridge and the A335. There is a bus stop close by, and the Old Beams public house, which provides excellent food, is a short walk to the right (south).

Adjacent to the inn and behind the post box is a thatched cottage at right angles to the road. Originally called Halfway Cottage, probably because it marks the half-way point between Fordingbridge and Ringwood, it is now called Thatched Eaves. It is immortalised as the thatched cottage featured on the lid of Cadbury's Dairy Box chocolates, on numerous jigsaw puzzles and wrapping paper. It forms one of a row of thatched cottages which overlook the river. The Old Beams inn formed a part of this until 1934. It is interesting to note that these are thatched with the original Hampshire thatch ridge. This is a simple method of finishing the ridge by wrapping the wheat straw over the ridge and holding it in place with hazel spars and not embossing it in any way. In this area it was also common to wrap heather round the waistcoats – the larch poles beneath the thatch – as it was readily available from the Forest. There is a choice of two materials for the thatch, either wheat or reed; the latter used to be obtained from the reed beds of the Solent or Christchurch Harbour. If reeds were used, the ridge would generally be made from sedge spears cut from the river bank as these are pliable and could be bent into place.

FORDINGBRIDGE to IBSLEY
4 MILES

Public Transport
Bus Service from:
Salisbury to Bournemouth X3
Salisbury to Swanage X81, Sundays in summer only

Where to Park
A large free central car park.

Where to Stay
Accommodation list from the Tourist Information Office, Main Car Park, Lyndhurst, Hants SO43 7NY   Tel. (01703) 282269 or from the Tourist Information Office, Salisbury Street, Fordingbridge, Hants SP6 1AB Tel. (01425) 654560, open Easter to September only.
Lions Court Restaurant and Hotel, 29 High Street, Fordingbridge Tel. (01425) 652006
The Ship Inn, High Street, Fordingbridge Tel. (01425) 652776
Sandy Balls Estate Holiday Centre, Fordingbridge Tel. (01425) 653042
Red Shoot Camping Park, Linwood, Nr Ringwood BH24 1AZ Tel. (01425) 473789, March to October.

Where to Eat
There are pubs, bakeries, take-away shops and a small supermarket in Fordingbridge.
Belinda's Bakery, Fordingbridge
The George Inn, Fordingbridge
The Old Beams Inn, Ibsley Tel. (01425) 473387

Places to Visit
St Mary's Church, Fordingbridge
Bicton Mill trout farm

Directions
For those arriving by public transport the bus stop is outside the Post Office. Walk south to the mini-roundabout at the junction with Bridge Street. Turn right into the High Street.

Leaving the car park by the eastern entrance near the toilets leads to the High Street.

Continue along the High Street for about 200 yds. At the fork in the road take the left hand fork into Provost Street. Cross the river and continue to the left into Church Street.

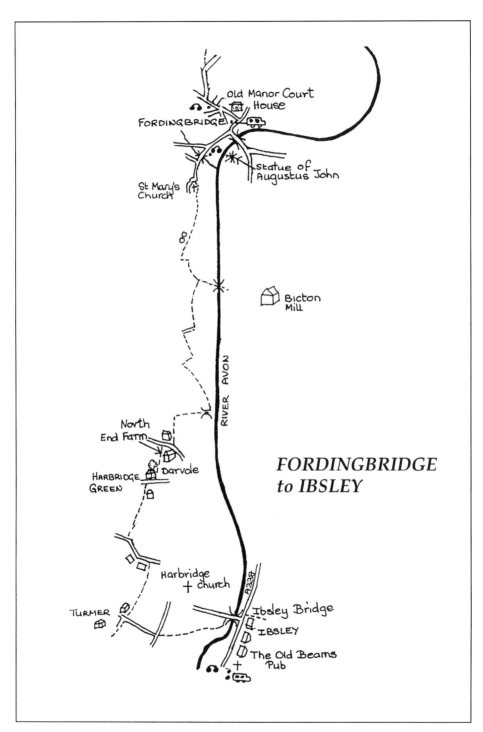

Old Manor Court House

FORDINGBRIDGE

statue of Augustus John

St Mary's Church

Bicton Mill

RIVER AVON

North End Farm

Darvole

HARBRIDGE GREEN

FORDINGBRIDGE to IBSLEY

Harbridge + church

TURMER

A338

Ibsley Bridge

IBSLEY

The Old Beams Pub

The path crosses the churchyard and leaves the town along a grass path, eventually passing the sewage works on the right. Cross a small bridge and a metal kissing gate. Cross this field to the south-east corner, walk across a second footbridge and follow the right hand field boundary hedge for 50 yds to another stile into a field on the right. From this point it is possible to reach Bicton by following the footpath straight ahead.

Cross the old irrigation channels on this field heading south. The path keeps to the right hand field boundary to cross a couple of stiles until it turns right (west) onto a tree-lined farm track and after about 150 yds, cross two stiles in quick succession. The stream, which may be dry in summer, forms the left hand boundary of this field. Follow the stream south to the next stile, and on to another stile after which turn right to follow the right-hand field boundary west and then south. Here the stream is on the right. Cross another stile and footbridge into an area of reed beds. Turn right across a large wooden bridge over Midgeham drain (with handrails made by Hampshire County Council in 1989 as part of the Avon Valley Footpath) and then along a board-walk into the corner of a field. Walk uphill, following the left hand field boundary away from the river and turn left onto a farm track which heads south to North End Farm.

At the junction with the metalled road, turn right. Follow the road for 100 yds uphill. Just beyond North End Farmhouse turn left across a stile. Continue south across two fields and turn left at the stile under a spreading oak tree to the rear of a thatched house. Cross over a footbridge and follow the path beside a private garden. A stile leads into a metalled road. Turn right to the hamlet of Harbridge Green. Follow the road for 50 yds and opposite Darvole, a thatched house, turn left down a gravel track following a stream for 400 yds.

At Cobley Cottage, at the end of the track, bear right to the stile and then left (south-west) following the stream on the left. At the metalled road, turn left (south-east) towards Harbridge. After 300 yds, just beyond a small brick cottage, turn right across a stile in the hedge into a field and proceed south straight across to a second stile into the next field. Follow a small copse on the right and continue following the right hand boundary towards Harbridge Farm. Cross a stile into the farm drive and walk down to the village green and duck pond. Turn left along the gravel road (east) towards the river. Where the road bends to the left, take the path straight ahead through the kissing gate and over a bridge into the water meadows. Cross a series of stiles, following the river bank east against the flow of the river to the distant Ibsley Bridge.

Section 6
IBSLEY TO RINGWOOD
5 MILES

From Ibsley Bridge, the footpath leads eastward across arable land to the old medieval road which ran from village to village along the gravel terrace to the east of the valley. It then crosses grazing land to the edge of Summerlug Hill, where it turns south and follows the edge of Ibsley Common. Although shown as being within the Forest boundaries, commoners' rights rather than foresters' hold sway here. These are more prized by the locals, as they apply to individuals and not just to the property. They cover the free grazing of sheep, cattle and ponies, the digging of sand, gravel and soil, the cutting of turf, bracken and heather and the pulling up of trees. They do not allow the cutting of trees, the digging of sandstone, shooting or fishing.

It is near here in Gorley that Heywood Sumner lived at Cuckoo Hill. He describes in his books the Great Fire of 1906 which raged across the common. Happily, it recovered, and today the curlews fly up from the coastal areas to nest in the boggy patches during the month of May. The nightjars can also be seen in May and June, fallow deer are often spotted, as are grass snakes, slow worms, smooth snakes, lizards and the occasional adder. Walking along the edge of the common just above the spring line where the gravel layer above gives way to the clay below, watch out for the change in vegetation from the ling heather above, to the moisture-loving cross-leaved heather and sedge grass below. Where the springs rise, so the cotton grass grows. To avoid a repeat of the 'Great Fire' and to prevent the land from becoming furze-sick, growth of the bracken, heather and gorse are carefully controlled by regular burning.'

Beyond Summerlug Hill the path drops down to cross a 'droke' at **Mockbeggar** (drokes are the small valleys leading off the forest plain). Across the stream the route continues round Ibsley Common. From this point there are views across the valley to Somerley House in the far distance. In the near distance can be seen the wartime remains of Ibsley Airfield, which was opened in February 1941. It was commissioned as a satellite to Middle Wallop but soon became a front line air base. No. 32 Squadron arrived first with their Hurricanes, but no sooner had they arrived than they were attacked by the German Luftwaffe, which dropped 30 bombs, damaging at least one aeroplane. After a couple of months they were replaced by No. 118 Squadron of Spitfires, whose mission was to provide escort to the convoys coming up the Channel. Notably they escorted both the king and Churchill back home from North Africa. By D-Day, it was a American air base which was used on the day to provide convoy and beach cover. The airfield continued in use after the war,

Crossing a droke at Mockbeggar.

but it was finally closed in 1947, to be used briefly as a race track. It was also used once as a location for a film starring David Niven, who stayed in Ibsley village.

The path drops down to the minor road leading to **Moyles Court**, once the home of Dame Alicia Lisle, whose husband John Lisle was responsible for the sentencing and execution of Colonel Penruddock of Hale House and as one of Cromwell's newly elected judges presided over the trial of King Charles I. This was to seal the fate of the elderly widow in 1685 after the Monmouth Rebellion.

Dame Alicia had been in London throughout the rebellion, which ended when Charles II's favourite illegitimate son, the Protestant Duke of Monmouth, was beaten by his Roman Catholic uncle, James II at the Battle of Sedgemoor on 6 July 1685. The Duke and a party of his men escaped towards Ringwood. Two of these men, John Hicks and Richard Nelthorpe, knowing that Dame Alicia was both kindly and a staunch Protestant, wrote to her asking for shelter. Dame Alicia, unsuspecting of their involvement in the rebellion, welcomed them into her home. News of their arrival reached the ears of Colonel Penruddock's son, who immediately saw a way to avenge his father's death and informed the King's men. Dame Alicia realised her mistake too late; before she could have the men removed they were all arrested and taken to Winchester to appear before Judge Jeffryes and his Bloody Assize.

At the trial Judge Jeffryes bullied the jury until they found Dame Alicia guilty and then he sentenced her to be burnt alive. The clergy at Winchester and the people of Hampshire were outraged at the sentence and demanded that she should be treated more leniently, as was appropriate to her age. The judge, fearful for his safety when crossing Hampshire on his way to the West Country and not wishing to alienate the clergy, referred the case to the King, who also saw a chance to avenge the death of his father. King James demanded that Dame Alicia should die, but agreed to execution by beheading. So, on 2 September 1685 Dame Alicia was beheaded in the Market Place in Winchester and her body was brought back to the church at Ellingham for a decent burial.

The route continues across Dockens Water and south past the Alice Lisle pub

Ford over Dockens Water.

to the corner of Ivy Lane, from where it winds its way between the old water-filled gravel pits to Ringwood. These lakes are the result of the gravel extraction which has been carried out in this part of the Avon Valley since 1938. The lakes are now used for recreational purposes. The first to be passed is Spinnaker Lake, home of the sailing club. The path then follows the artificially raised banks of the Lin Brook as it winds its way between Linbrook Lake and Kingfisher Lake, both used for trout fishing.

After passing beneath the A31, the route continues along Gravel Lane, past the Manor House on the left, once the home of Lord Chief Justice William Murray, Earl of Mansfield and, more recently towards the end of the nineteenth century, of Dowager Lady Morant, whose family owned Ringwood until 1916.

The path crosses the Furlong car park to the tourist information office and the bus stops on the far side.

IBSLEY to RINGWOOD
5 MILES

Public Transport
Bus service from:
Salisbury to Bournemouth X3
Salisbury to Swanage, Sundays in summer only, X81

Where to Park
Parking for a few cars to the west of Ibsley Bridge
Parking on the slip road outside the Old Beams Inn

Where to Stay
Accommodation list from the Tourist Information Office, main car park, Lyndhurst, Hants SO43 7N. Tel. (01703) 282269
The Tourist Information Office, The Furlong, Ringwood, Hants BH24 3QT. Tel. (01425) 470896. Easter to September only.
Candlestick Cottage Restaurant and Lodge, 136 Christchurch Road, Ringwood, Hants BH24 3AP Tel. (01425) 472587
Original White Hart Hotel, Market Place, Ringwood, Hants BH24 1AW Tel. (01425) 472702
Moortown Lodge Hotel and Restaurant, 244 Christchurch Road, Ringwood, Hants BH24 3AS Tel. (01425) 471404 Fax (01425) 476052
Red Shoot Camping Park, Linwood, near Ringwood BH24 1AZ Tel. (01425) 473789, March to October.
Nags Head Camp Site, Moortown, Ringwood. Tel. 01452 473263

Where to Eat
There are pubs, bakeries, take away shops and supermarkets in Ringwood.
Belinda's Bakery, The High Street, Ringwood
The Peppercorn Restaurant, Meeting House Lane, Ringwood
Framptons Mill, The Furlong, Ringwood
Old Cottage Restaurant, West Street, Ringwood
The Original White Hart, The Market Place, Ringwood
The Old Beams Inn, Ibsley
Ice cream van at the ford by Moyles Court School

Places to Visit
The Meeting House, The Furlong, Ringwood

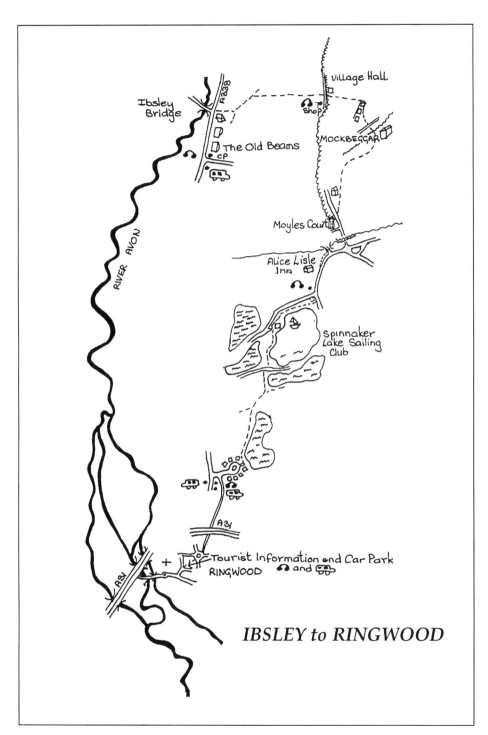

Ibsley Bridge

A338

The Old Beams

CP

RIVER AVON

Village Hall

Shop

MOCKBEGGAR

Moyles Court

Alice Lisle Inn

Spinnaker Lake Sailing Club

A31

A31

Tourist Information and Car Park

RINGWOOD and

IBSLEY to RINGWOOD

Directions

From the bridge, cross the main road with care to a narrow path on the left of the entrance of Bridge Farm leading to a stile. Cross two fields. Follow the left hand field boundary to the stile in the corner and turn left (north) keeping the field boundary to the right until the path crosses a stile through the hedge. (At the time of printing, this section of the path is the subject of a temporary diversion order to allow gravel workings.) Please follow the waymarks. Should you encounter a problem, contact (01962) 846042.

Follow the right hand field boundary towards the Forest (east) through two fields to a stile leading onto a road. Cross the road and take the path (south) to the right of the village hall car park. Keep to the hedge on the left, cross the next stile and continue uphill across two fields (east) where the path brings you out in front of a redbrick chalet bungalow. Turn right (south) over the stile and follow a path diagonally up, via a board-walk through the wood and round Summerlug Hill for about 100 yds. Take a right turn down through the trees to the gravel lane below. Cross the lane and descend to the stream. Cross the wooden footbridge and continue to the edge of the forest, keeping close to the field boundary on the right (south).

At the end of the path before Newlands Plantation, descend to the right and locate a stile in the corner of the open heathland. The path leads behind a bungalow downhill across two fields and stiles to the gate onto the road. Turn left and follow the wide grass verge past Moyles Court and over the ford at Dockens Water. From the ford follow the road to the right and at the next road junction bear left. Cross the Ellingham Road to the stile in the corner of the field. Turn left and follow the path parallel to the road until you reach the Alice Lisle public house. Cross the green in front of the pub and continue over the cattle grid, passing the telephone box and Ivy Lane. Just beyond Ivy Cottage, take the path to the right via the bridle gate. Follow the path around Spinnaker Lake and along the back of the sailing club car park. Turn right and follow the path until it meets Ivy Lane, turn left here and continue along the path between hedges with Spinnaker Lake on the left and Blashford Lake on the right. There are several benches along here – a good picnic spot. The metal kissing gate at the end of the path leads onto Snails Lane. Turn right at Snails Lane and after 50 yds turn left through another metal kissing gate. Follow the path which bends to the right. Keep the stream (Dockens Water) on your left and cross the concrete footbridge and continue along the path, now keeping the stream on the right. Continue following the path until it enters a housing estate. Take either road round a grassed circle and turn left into Linbrook Court. Cross Northfield Road into Gravel Lane. Pass under the A31 and continue into Ringwood.

Just before the roundabout, cross the dual carriageway. Take the footpath on the left which crosses the car park diagonally to the information centre, bus stops and toilets.

Section 7
RINGWOOD

Cheer up, my brave Comrades, today is our own!
We've fought a good fight for our jolly old town,
and shewn to her friends and her foes one and all
to herself, if she's faithfull, she never shall fall.

These words from the town song were penned in 1830, when the Old Mill at Bickerley came under attack from the people of Fordingbridge during the machine riots of the agricultural depression. Since Ringwood was first established as an ancient river crossing, road junction and Roman trading post, the people of Ringwood have had to struggle to survive. Even today the town struggles against becoming a satellite to Bournemouth, Christchurch and Poole.

In the early days Ringwood was separated from large centres of population by the surrounding areas of barren heathland. It was called Rimuc Wude by the Saxons, translated as 'Edge of Wood' and in the Domesday Book it is referred to as Rincvede, meaning ford over the river. Ringwood developed as a typical Anglo-Saxon village with two large fields on either side, north field and east field, with Eastfield Lane and Northfield Lane leading back into the village centre. These fields were each made up of several hundred 'strips', which were a unit of cultivation measuring approximately an acre, 220 yds by 22 yds. A bundle or parcel of these strips all running in the same direction was called a furlong. The Furlong car park was once part of the agricultural land surrounding the village. It was known as Butt's Furlong before the bypass was built in 1978 and the pasture land disappeared under tarmac.

The village became a market town in 1226 when Henry III granted it a charter to hold a produce market every Wednesday. It was not until 1553 that Edward VI granted it permission to have a cattle market, and then the cattle were tied up to the church wall and the ponies were trotted up and down the High Street to be put through their paces.

In 1337 Ringwood was granted the right to hold two fairs: one on St Andrew's Day (30 November) and one on St Peter's Day (29 June). The fairs were the busiest days of the year, with buyers coming from all over the country and gypsies camping on Butt's Furlong. The shop windows along the High Street were boarded up against the surging mass of animals and the street fights which broke out amongst the gypsies. It is reported that on one occasion at least 12 policemen were brought in to control the crowds. During the fairs much beer was drunk, Ringwood being famous for its strong ale. Nowadays the fairs and the animal markets are a thing of the past, although the town does still hold a carnival every September, when the procession of carnival floats can stretch for at least a mile and it is still attended by numerous policemen to control the crowds.

The brewing of beer was once so common in Ringwood that the town was described in 1898 thus: 'Old Ringwood seems all Malthouses and breweries, and the strong heavy liquor was drunk everywhere, even horse pond water was used and the leaves of bog myrtle substituted in place of hops.' In truth, the breweries used barley grown on the nearby chalk uplands, hops which were grown in hop gardens around Ringwood and north-east Hampshire and water drawn from the river. Ale is an old English word for a period of merrymaking when beer was drunk and Ales were held to celebrate all manner of occasions, the most well known today being the wedding feast or bride-ale corrupted to bridal and the Church Ale which became known as the local, a term we now use for the inn. Ringwood was not short of these; by 1855 there were no fewer than 20 inns in the town, many of which still exist today. Opposite the tourist information office is the Inn on the Furlong, owned by the present Ringwood Brewery.

Beside the Inn on the Furlong is the old Unitarian Meeting House, built in 1727, which is now used as the Local History Museum. It is one of the best pre-served eighteenth-century dissenting meeting houses, still in its original condition, with box pews and a gallery on three sides.

Walk down Meeting House Lane to the Market Place. On a Wednesday morning it will be alive with all the excitement of the market. On other days of the week it is quiet and it is possible to see many of the fine buildings surrounding the square. These buildings reflect the years of prosperity during the eighteenth century when Ringwood traded with Newfoundland through the port of Poole. Beer, cloth and animal traps were exchanged for seal skins, processed in the tanneries at Bickerley.

The first building on the right at the end of Meeting House Lane is the old town hall and corn exchange. This was built by John Morant in 1868, but its function as a corn exchange was short lived, owing to the agricultural depression. It was converted into a cinema before its present use was established as a shopping arcade. Continuing along the street on the right is one of Ringwood's oldest inns, the original White Hart. The name is said to stem from a visit of Henry VII to the town. Local legend tells us that he had a memorable chase of a white stag called Albert, which finally turned at bay on the water meadows outside town. The ladies of the party pleaded that he should be spared, so the King called off his hounds and hung a gold chain around the young stag's neck. The King is then reported to have returned to the inn to sample some of the town's beer. The inn commemorated the event by hanging a picture of the stag outside as a sign. This is an alternative to the usual story that Edward IV, who wore a badge depicting a white hart wearing a gold chain, took a particular interest in the highways of the realm and the provision of posting houses. As a result, many houses were built during his reign and took as their sign his

The inn on the Furlong.

insignia. However, most of these establishments were built along main roads, and indeed there is another White Hart in Ringwood on the Southampton road, which was the main road to London before the bypass.

Beyond is a building with a fine pillared portico and Venetian window. This building was the Crown Inn and staging post for the Avon Coach which left regularly for Salisbury and for the many coaches going to London. In 1801 the inn moved to its present site, and the original building became the Ringwood and Hampshire Bank and home of Steven Turk, a local businessman who also owned a brewery and seven inns in town.

Continue across the market-place past the present church of St Peter and St Paul which dates from 1853, and turn down West Street towards the river. On the right is Monmouth House, where the Duke of Monmouth was held after his capture near Horton. It was from this house that he wrote letters to his uncle, King James II, begging forgiveness and pleading for his life. His pleas fell on deaf ears, for he was taken to London and was beheaded on Tower Hill.

The route passes a terrace of thatched cottages (now the Old Cottage

Restaurant) and down to the river bank at Jubilee Gardens. At Ringwood the river divides, and from the gardens it is possible to see the small bridge taking the road across the mill stream and the larger three-arched bridge called Stoning Bridge.

From Jubilee Gardens the path leaves the centre of Ringwood and follows the mill stream towards the **Bickerley**. A terrace of Victorian villas on the right of the path was built on the site of the old tannery, which closed in 1875 and covered an area of 2 acres.

The Old Mill flats on the left was once the site of the Old Mill which had been used as a fulling mill from 1667. There was a thriving textile industry until the 1780s, after which competition was too great from the West Country and later the great textile mills of the north. During the eighteenth and nineteenth centuries there had been a prosperous domestic industry in the town making stockings, collars and cuffs and hand-knitted gloves. These latter were made using a stitch peculiar to the town and sold nationally as Ringwoods. At one time over 900 people were employed in the business. But in the 1950s, cheap imports from Japan and Hong Kong made it uneconomic to continue in production.

From the Bickerley, the path continues south and crosses the disused railway line. This line, which opened in 1847, linked Southampton to Wimborne and Poole. In 1862 a branch line opened between Ringwood and Christchurch. Both lines were superseded by the new London to Bournemouth line which brought holiday makers to the new seaside resort and led to the closure of the station at Ringwood.

However, the presence of the station was of great importance to the town and accounted in part for the establishment of the J.J. Armfield's Vale of Avon Ironworks, which produced milling and agricultural machinery. In 1876 they operated from the site of the present Ringwood Brewery. In 1890 a new foundry was built across the road closer to the station. Cheap coal, coke and iron ore were brought by ship to Poole and then by rail to Ringwood, where the ironworks was able to begin the manufacture of the British Empire turbines which were to replace the old water-wheels in mills, not only in the Avon Valley but around the world. Mill machinery manufactured in Ringwood is found as far away as Australia, India and Africa and water pumps in such places as Jamaica, Egypt and Mauritius. In 1910 they started the manufacture of turbines to produce electricity, which were particularly suitable for use on rivers where there was a low head of water. These were installed at Downton and Ringwood, where in 1924, the Ringwood Electricity Supply Company installed two Armfield river patent turbines with an output of 72 kilowatts. Eventually these were attached to the National Grid system until the mill closed in 1960.

J.J. Armfield's metalworks also produced cast iron used in the production of lamp posts, railings, road signs and farmers' ploughs. Sand excavated from a pit on Hightown Hill just to the east of the town beside the A31 and brought down on horse-drawn wagons was used in the casting process. In 1930 they began making car parts for Wellworthy's Lymington Garage Company, to whom the company was sold in 1943. As the path passes the end of the David Lloyd Centre, with its tennis courts and club house, it is an interesting thought that this was originally the Wellworthy's social club.

The path continues for a short distance alongside the river described here by Robert Southey:

> Nor fraught with merchant wealth, nor famed in song
> This river rolls an unobtrusive tide
> Its gentle charms may soothe and satisfy thy feelings.

As at Salisbury, the river at Ringwood was never successfully used for navigational purposes. James Taylor stopped here on his way up river in his wherry and was welcomed to the town by a fanfare played by the local band. Any works undertaken to make the river navigable following the 1664 Navigation Act were washed away by the severe floods of 1687. In 1730 plans that had been intended to make Ringwood an inland port were finally abandoned and the river was used thereafter solely for pleasure craft. In 1907 the ancient public rights to sail boats on the river were denied by the fishing and riparian interests, and although the case was brought before the High Court, there was not enough money to pursue it successfully.

Section 8
RINGWOOD TO SOPLEY
6.5 MILES

From Hampshire Hatches on the outskirts of Ringwood the path winds across **Kingston Common**, where soldiers camped during the First World War. To the east of the B3347 to Christchurch is the site of Bisterne Airfield, used briefly during the Second World War by the American 371st Fighter Group to carry out dive bombing attacks on trains, airfields and lines of communication in northern France in readiness for the D-Day invasion. The runways were constructed of wire mesh, and after the invasion all trace of the landing ground was quickly removed, allowing it to revert immediately to farmland.

After passing to the west of the house at Kingston, the path rejoins the B3347 near the football pitches south of Dragon Cottages. These formed part of the Green Dragon Inn until 1878. The cottages, situated at the end of Dragon Lane and close to Dragon Field, are named after the Burley Dragon which reputedly roamed this area in 1431. The dragon was believed to have its den at Burley Beacon 5 miles away, and every morning it flew to Bisterne for a drink of milk which was put out by the villagers. Eventually the inhabitants of **Bisterne**

Kingston

wished to be rid of the dragon and Sir Maurice Berkeley of Berkeley Castle in Gloucester, and also owner of Bisterne Manor, built himself a hide in the Dragon Field and with his two dogs lay in wait. It is said that the Sir Maurice's armour was covered with broken glass stuck on with holly sap, known as a protection against dragons. The dragon was slain, and to this day, stone mastiffs grace the second floor pediment on the front of Bisterne Manor as a reminder of the dogs' courageous fight. The family crest above the door still depicts a dragon and a beacon. It is likely that there is some truth in the story, but the dragon would most likely have been a wolf. Bisterne Manor, clearly visible from the road, was probably remodelled in 1652, the date on the coat of arms.

Beyond Bisterne Manor there are views to the west across the Avon Valley to Matchams House, perched high on the ridge above the river. The house was built in the early nineteenth century by George Matcham, husband of Lord Nelson's elder sister, Catherine. Today it is a leisure centre with, among other things, a night club and race tracks for stock cars and go-carts.

As one walks along the road trying to ignore the traffic it is worth reflecting that in 1937 a census of vehicles using the road estimated a figure of 9271 vehicles per week, roughly the number that use it each hour today.

South of Lower Bisterne Farm the path turns east to pass behind the Avon Tyrrell hotel, where Sir Walter Tyrrell reputedly stopped in his flight from the New Forest after the slaying of William Rufus. At the nearby smithy he had his horse shod, arranging for the shoes to be put on back to front to confuse his pursuers. He then set out to cross the Avon and so escape from the country.

A short walk across open fields to the banks of Sopley Brook and then beside the stream through Vatchers Common to **Sopley**: on the left bank of Sopley Brook is the site of another temporary wartime airfield known as Winkton Airfield, which served as an advanced landing ground for the American 404th Fighter Group which flew P47 Thunderbolts, providing air cover for the D-Day invasion. Beforehand they were used to locate and destroy buzz bomb sites. It too was abandoned after D-Day and quickly reverted to agricultural use.

On reaching Sopley, the path follows the B3347 into the village, passing a modern blacksmith on the left, where trade has continued for at least a hundred years. The one-way system was first introduced in 1938.

The Woolpack is a pretty thatched pub, built as a cottage with a wool store in 1725 and used as an inn since 1783, adopting the name from the bag that sheeps' fleeces are kept in. It is now a very popular pub serving good food and at weekends can be extremely busy.

In a corner of the garden opposite the Woolpack car park was the village laundry. Using water pumped from Sopley Brook, Mrs Barrow and several employees worked their way through several large wheelbarrow loads of laundry from Sopley House each week. It is said that throughout the week the bushes along the road would be bedecked with washing drying in the fresh air, and at the end of the week Mrs Barrow would dress up her donkey Jane, hitch up the cart and set out to make her delivery to the 'big house', returning via the village hostelries.

It is worthwhile making a short detour from the path along the lane opposite the Woolpack to the church of St Michael and All Angels and the mill. The church is built on a high mound above the tidal waters of the Avon and may be on the site of a pagan temple. Alternatively, it may have been a base for the Jute invaders who came up river from Christchurch and were known to raise moots and to use the rivers as routes into the interior. Parts of the church date from the eleventh century, but mostly it was built of rubble ironstone in the thirteenth century.

At the end of the lane is the mill, close to the church both geographically and in importance. The mill probably predates the church and gains a mention in the Domesday Book. Unlike most of the mills on the river, it was exclusively a corn mill throughout its history. In 1878 the wheel was replaced with a 12-horsepower turbine by Mr Beminster, the then miller. He also added the third floor for corn storage. The mill now houses a restaurant with wonderful views across the valley and 'dismal swamp'.

I am told that in the late 1970s the river from Mudeford to Sopley was brought alive once more by the Mudeford Lifeboat crew, who dressed up as smugglers and re-enacted a smuggling run, rowing upriver with their boats loaded with tubs. At Sopley the men were apprehended by the local villagers dressed as militia men, and a battle ensued which at times became rather too realistic. The day ended with a mock trial presided over by the local magistrate, a timely reminder that contraband was brought up river to Sopley and then across land to Burley and beyond.

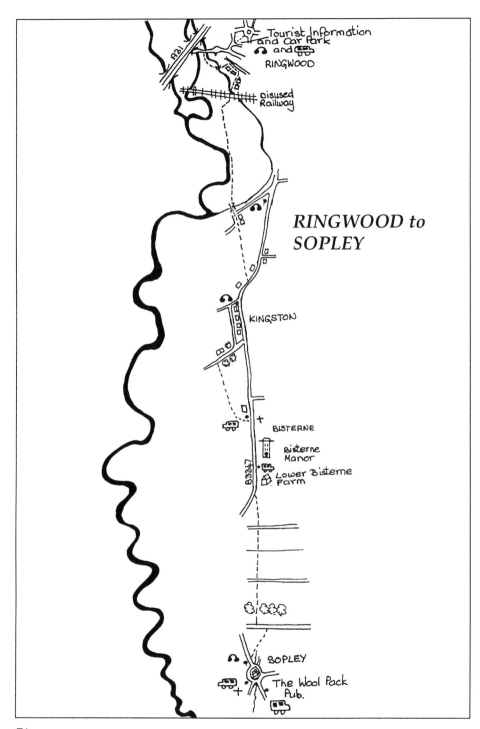

RINGWOOD to SOPLEY

RINGWOOD to SOPLEY

6.5 MILES

Public Transport
Bus service from:
Salisbury to Bournemouth, X3
Salisbury to Swanage, Sundays in summer only, X81
Southampton to Bournemouth, X1, X2
Southampton to Poole, 180
Lyndhurst to Ringwood, X1
Christchurch to Ringwood, 105, 115, not Sundays or bank holidays
Milford-on-Sea to Ringwood, X31, summer only
National Express Tel. (0990) 808080
Excelsior Coaches Tel. (01202) 396655

Where to Park
Large car park in the centre of Ringwood

Where to Stay
Accommodation list from the Tourist Information Office, Main Car Park, Lyndhurst, Hants SO43 7NY Tel. (01703) 282269
The Tourist Information Office, The Furlong, Ringwood, Hants BH24 3QT. Tel. (01425) 470890. Open Easter to October only.
The Tourist Information Office, The High Street, Christchurch, Hants Tel. (01202) 471780
Original White Hart Hotel, Market Place, Ringwood, Hants BH24 1AW Tel. (01425) 47202/473313
Moortown Lodge Hotel and Restaurant, 244 Christchurch Road, Ringwood, Hants BH24 3AS Tel. (01425) 471404 Fax (01425) 476052
Nags Head Camp Site, Moortown, Ringwood Tel. (01425) 473263

Where to Eat
There are pubs, bakeries, take-away shops and supermarkets in Ringwood.
Belinda's Bakery, The High Street, Ringwood
The Peppercorn Restaurant, Meeting House Lane, Ringwood
Framptons Mill, The Furlong, Ringwood
Old Cottage Restaurant, West Street, Ringwood
Original White Hart Hotel, Market Place, Ringwood
The Wool Pack, Sopley

Places to Visit
The Meeting House, The Furlong, Ringwood

Directions

From the tourist information centre turn right past the Furlong public house and into Meeting House Lane, which leads to the High Street. Turn right to the Market Square. Pass the Original White Hart public house and bear left into West Street, pass Monmouth House and the Old Cottage Restaurant to the river. Cross the bridge and immediately take the path on the left beside the tackle shop. Pass through a small residential mobile home park to a stile which leads into the water meadows. Cross to the mill stream and take the footbridge to the left bank of Bickerley Common.

Turn right along a gravel drive in front of a row of terraced cottages. Beyond the last cottage, turn right. Keep to the gravel track which passes five semi-detached houses on the left. Take the right fork and continue straight ahead over the disused railway line and over a stile into the meadows. The path leads to the right along a boardwalk to a stile beside a metal field gate. Beyond the stile, turn left and follow the left hand field boundary to an old gate post. From here, continue straight ahead across the meadows to a waymarker post in the middle of the next field about 200 yds away. This indicates that the path takes a left turn. Head towards the reed beds on the left and there is a wooden board-walk under the willow trees.

Cross the next meadow to the right-hand end of a row of willows on the boundary of the Sports Club. From here, walk over a sluice gate and along the river bank for 100 yds. The path then turns left away from the river, to a stile which leads to a narrow footpath between hawthorn hedges. At the end of the track, cross three bridges, and at the junction with the tarmac road follow the gravel track to the right, away from the mill stream between hedges. Cross over a cattle grid and take the right hand gravel fork. Pass two cottages on the left opposite common land and after 200 yds, at a T junction with a gravel track, take the grass track opposite. Continue across the common. The path bends to the left and through a gateway to cross a stile. Continue along the grass track, keeping to the left hand boundary, then over a stile onto an old grass path which continues between hedges to another stile. A further stile leads into a field. Cross this to a stile leading onto the main Ringwood–Christchurch Road.

Turn right and before the telephone box turn right again along a surfaced lane, then left onto a gravel track which continues for some distance passing Parkwood Engineering. Where the gravel track turns left continue straight ahead onto a grass track leading after 70 yds to a tree-lined lane. Pass cottages on the right and immediately turn left. Follow the field boundary on the left to a path between two fields. This path leads across a stile into a sunken gully, ending at a gate opening onto the road.

Turn right opposite Bisterne Church and walk along the verge for $3/4$ mile, continue past Lower Bisterne Farm on the left and take a path on the left. The path bends to the right to a tarmac lane. Cross via the kissing gates and cross the wide flat field behind the Avon Tyrrell Hotel to the next farm track. Cross several fields and at the third surfaced lane beyond a stile beside a gateway, turn left for 50 yds to the bridge. Turn right before the bridge through a kissing gate and follow the stream, then the field boundary, then the stream again, crossing a series of stiles to the main road. Turn left to Sopley. Continue down the one way system in the reverse direction to the Woolpack Inn.

Section 9
SOPLEY TO CHRISTCHURCH
3.5 MILES

Looking downstream from the bridge at the Woolpack, there is a modern water pumping station; it was here on Butters Moor that two water rams powered by natural springs once pumped water to Sopley House and the goldfish pond in the park. Beside the entrance to the house is a drinking fountain similar to that seen at Turmer.

Sopley House was demolished in 1988. It had been rebuilt in 1790 by its owner, James Compton, who became very well known in the area as a keen sheep farmer. With the vicar, the Reverend Mr Willis, he was responsible for introducing Merino sheep into the area. This Spanish breed of sheep gave very fine soft wool which was much sought after, and **Sopley** became an important specialist wool producing area.

In 1834 the house was bought by John Kemp-Welch, a London merchant and owner of Schweppes. The house was noted for its three stained glass windows depicting the story of Sir Walter Tyrrell. When the house was sold again in 1885, the land was described thus: 'The arable land is a rich and productive loam and is chiefly what is known as good sheep and barley land. It is in a very high state of cultivation and we have seldom seen over land more even in quality or in better condition.'

In 1918 there was a horrific accident on the lawns of Sopley House. Lieutenant Barrington, a pilot, landed his plane in front of the house to ask for directions. As he got out, a crowd gathered and he enlisted the help of several onlookers to hold the plane while he swung the propeller. As the engine started, the helpers were unable to hold the plane, which shot away across the grass, until it eventually tipped up and came to a halt. Not, however, before one person had been killed by the propeller and another had been run over, although miraculously he escaped unhurt.

The path skirts the old coach house and crosses the fields to Staple Cross. Once past the Lamb inn, the path follows the stream to **Burton**.

Burton Hall is a fine Georgian house built of red brick in 1750. In recent times it has been used as a country club, but now its land has been built on and a modern housing estate stretches to Stoney Lane and the water meadows beside the river. It was from a thatched cottage called Burton Cottage, on the left hand corner of the path as it turns west to cross the estate, that Robert Southey, who became poet laureate later in life, looked across the valley to the river and St Catherine's Hill beyond, and wrote his *English Eclogues*.

The beauty of the place, yon healthy hill
That rises sudden from the vales so green.

In 1797 Robert Southey and his young bride came to Burton from London where he had been studying law, and stayed until 1799, when ill health drove him to Portugal. On his arrival at Burton he wrote, 'This New Forest is simply lovely. I should like to have a house in it and dispeople the rest like the conqueror.' At first he found rooms in Burton, but later he was to take the lease on Burton Cottage; at the time it was two small cottages which he had converted into one and was to refer to as his palace.

He was visited there by Charles Lamb, and would often walk across the meadows to Mudeford, where William Stuart Rose, MP for Christchurch and himself a poet and traveller, had recently built a most unusual house on the sea front called Gundimore. Many other well known poets and writers of the day were invited to visit here, including Robert Southey's brother-in-law, Samuel Coleridge and Sir Walter Scott, who wrote *Marmion* in the house.

Whilst at Burton Southey wrote several poems, but arguably his best works are not his poems but his prose, especially his *Life of Lord Nelson*, inspired, perhaps, not only by the events of the time, but by tales recounted by his brother in the cottage at Burton, of his experiences as one of Napoleon's prisoners.

Burton Cottage

From Burton the path crosses the water meadows and follows the river bank to Christchurch. These water meadows are a site of special scientific interest and an environmentally sensitive area. Plants such as arrowhead, flowering rush, water plantain and yellow iris are found here, reflecting the long history of traditional farming on these meadows. Diverse species of birds are attracted here throughout the year. Overwintering birds include snipe, redshank, white fronted geese and widgeon, and nesting birds in the spring include snipe and Lapwing. Mute swans and kingfishers are to be seen on the river, and along the river banks coots, moorhens, grey wagtails and warblers. Water crowfoot, spiked water milfoil and perfoliate pondweed grow alongside fringed water lilies and broad-leaved pondweed.

Inscription for a Tablet on the Banks of a Stream

Stranger awhile upon this mossy bank
Recline thee. If the sun rides high, the breeze,
That loves to ripple o'er the rivulet,
Will play around thou brow, and the cool sound,
Of running waters soothe thee. Mark how clear
It sparkles o'er the shallows, and behold
Where o'er its surface wheels with restless speed
Yon glossy insect, on the sand below
How the swift shadow flies. The stream is pure
In solitude, and many a healthful herb
Bends o'er its course and drinks the vital wave:
But passing on amid the haunts of man,
It finds pollution there, and rolls from thence
A tainted tide. Seek'st through for HAPPINESS?
Go stranger, sojourn in the woodland cot
Of INNOCENCE, and thou shalt find her there.

R. Southey

Across the meadows to the south is a wonderful view of Christchurch Priory, beyond the myriad electricity pylons.

A legend associated with the priory relates that when Ralph Flambard chose to build a fine new church on the summit of St Catherine's Hill, seen here across the river, there were mysterious powers at work to stop him. During the day, labourers toiled, carrying all the building materials to the top of the hill, and each night the materials were mysteriously removed and brought back down. Eventually work was abandoned and the church was built on its present site, which was a far more popular choice for the local inhabitants.

The path crosses the river at the Royalty Fisheries, so called because from the tenth century this was a royal manor under Edward the Confessor. The fishery

Water meadows towards Christchurch.

stretches from the first bend upstream of Knapp Mill to the harbour entrance. The coarse fishing on this stretch is still very good, with fresh water fish such as chub, perch, roach, dace, gudgeon, barbel, eels and salmon. Salmon are still caught here between 1 February and 30 September, although in recent years their numbers have declined. In 1990 just 104 were caught. The numbers of sea trout caught have also dropped in recent years; in 1980 there were 1500 compared with 50 in 1990. The barbel found in the river are not native to the Avon; they were introduced from the Thames in 1899 by the fishery owner at Iford on the Stour, and by 1911 had spread to the harbour and the Avon. The building on the weir is a disused eel house where, in 1955, 6000 eels, 1 ton in weight, were caught in the traps. The Royalty Fisheries are now owned by the West Hants Water Company based across the river on the site of the old Knapp Mill.

Knapp Mill was mentioned in the Domesday Book, where it is referred to as Chenap Mill in the manor of Hurn. It would originally have been a corn mill. In 1392 ownership passed to Christchurch Priory and in 1690 it was converted into a fulling mill. In 1760 it burnt down and was rebuilt as a corn mill. John Mills of Bisterne bought the mill in 1873 and it was acquired by the West Hants Water Company in 1895. They have since rebuilt it, destroying the old Saxon foundations in 1921. Water is extracted from the river here, to be pumped directly to Fawley or be purified for domestic use.

Many mills were converted for fulling in the sixteenth and seventeenth centuries when the wool trade was at is height. The spinning and weaving of the wool was a cottage industry and the cloth was later taken to the fuller to be cleansed and shrunk. Fuller's earth, a grey clay substance, was first used to remove the grease and then the cloth was placed in a gig to shrink it. The nap was raised by water-driven revolving drums of teasels. In 1568 Christchurch was famous for the manufacture of a frieze cloth, introduced by John Hastings from Haarlem in Holland, called Frizados. This was a coarse woollen cloth with a nap on one side only, and was used to make overcoats and suitings. It is thought that Knapp Mill played a part in its production.

The path continues alongside the river and under the railway bridge carrying the main Bournemouth to London train service. From the river, it turns west along Avon Buildings. In the 1840s this was known as Brewhouse Hole. The sanitation in Christchurch was very poor until 1902, when mains sewers were installed; until then, everything drained into the river. The privies were nearly always sited near wells, and as the soil in this area is very porous, the drinking water was soon contaminated. Smallpox and other diseases were rife in Christchurch and this area was a particularly unhealthy place to live. Beer became the most popular drink, as it was known to be safe, and from this time we have the expression small beer, meaning harmless and of little consequence. It is recorded that there were six breweries, 16 inns providing food, accommodation and spirits, and 26 alehouses providing beer in Christchurch. It was along Avon Buildings that they came with water carts from the nearby Frampton's Brewery to collect water from the river.

At the main road, the Electricity Museum can be found on the left. It was built in 1903 as the original electricity generating station for the public trams. It produced 500 volts of direct current from coal, brought from Portsmouth to the Town Quay by Mr Beminster's fleet of windjammers. Water was used from the river, which had been diverted for that purpose. At night the boilers were shut down, but there was enough excess electricity stored in batteries to illuminate the town. In the 1940s it became part of the National Grid.

Opposite the Electricity Museum behind Bargate Court, is Hart's factory, where fusee chains were made. This industry was first started in Christchurch by Robert Cox in 1790 from workshops in the High Street. Fusee chains were used in the gearing mechanism of watches. The cone-shaped gear was inspired by the spindle on a spinning wheel, known on the Continent as a Fuseau. Replacing gut with chain was the idea of M. Gruet of Geneva when he was in London in 1660. However, it was the Huguenots who brought the trade to England when they came in 1685. The work was so intricate – the chain's total thickness being only fourteen-hundredths of an inch, so fine that it could pass through the eye of a needle – that children as young as nine years were employed. After Britain and France went to war in 1793 Robert Cox had the monopoly on chain production in Britain, supplying watch, clock and chronometer makers throughout the country. Chain production flourished, and up to 400 women and children were employed. Hart's factory was built in 1845, using an advanced design with large glazed windows. In 1875 Swiss and American watches were made without the use of chains and demand fell. It was not long before the factory closed.

William Hart was also well known in the town as a taxidermist, who built up a huge collection of stuffed animals and birds, which he left to the town. Many of these can still be seen in the Red House Museum, which incidentally occupies the buildings of the old workhouse, near the Priory, from where so many of the fusee chain workers came.

In the centre of the road approaching the roundabout is a pink granite fountain incorporating a horse trough, a drinking fountain and water bowls for dogs beneath. This was raised to commemorate Samuel Beminster, who imported seed to the Town Quay and also the coal used by the Electricity Generating Station.

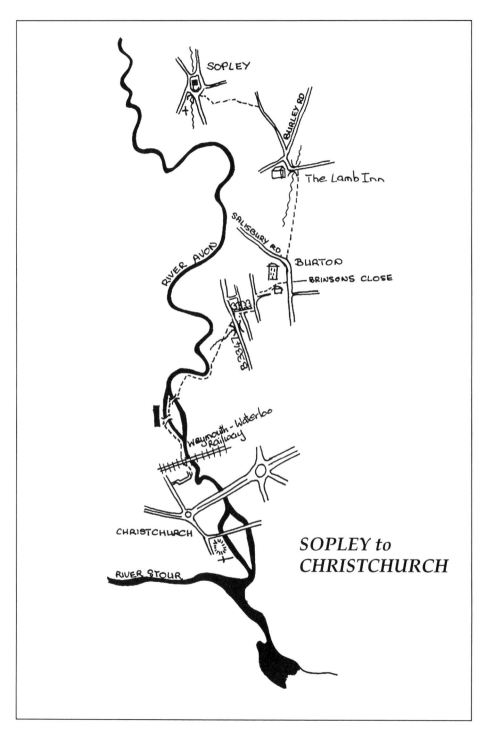

SOPLEY

BURLEY RD

The Lamb Inn

SALISBURY RD

RIVER AVON

BURTON

BRINSONS CLOSE

B3347

Weymouth - Waterloo Railway

CHRISTCHURCH

RIVER STOUR

SOPLEY to CHRISTCHURCH

SOPLEY to CHRISTCHURCH
3.5 MILES

Public Transport
Bus service from:
Christchurch to Ringwood, 105, 115 (not Sundays or Bank Holidays)

Where to Park
Beside the road leading to the church

Where to Stay
Accommodation list from The Tourist Information Office, The High Street, Christchurch, Hants Tel. (01202) 471780
The King's Arms Hotel, 18 Castle Street, Christchurch Tel. (01202) 484117
Three Gables, 11 Wickfield Avenue, Christchurch Tel. (01202) 481166

Where to Eat
The Woolpack, Sopley
Sopley Mill Restaurant, Sopley
Lamb Inn, Winkton
There are pubs, bakeries, take-away shops and supermarkets in Christchurch.

Places to Visit
Sopley Church
Christchurch Priory
Place Mill and Quay
Red House Museum and Gardens
Southern Electric Museum
Christchurch Tricycle Museum

Directions
Leaving the Woolpack Inn on the left, cross the bridge and the main Christchurch Road and go through the gates into Sopley Park. After 80 yds, go through an old metal kissing gate on the left and follow the enclosed path for a short distance parallel to the drive. Cross a stile into the field and follow the right hand boundary of the next field, passing a large house with a clock. Halfway along the field there is a stile on the right hand side. Cross diagonally to the next field to a stile, then diagonally across the next field. A further stile leads into a small copse and to a stile onto a tarmac lane.

Turn right and follow this lane to the crossroads at the Lamb Inn. (Going in the opposite direction it is all too easy to take the road to Bransgore, as the sign is very ambiguous. The correct lane is marked Ripley.) At the Lamb Inn turn left into Bockhampton Road between the pub and its car park. Follow the road with the stream on the left to the bridge. Just beyond the bridge, turn right and the path continues to follow the stream for $1/2$ mile to the road to Burton.

At the junction with the main road, cross over with care and turn left, passing Burton Hall on the right. Turn right just before a thatched house onto a path which leads into a housing estate. Follow the path through the housing estate down Brinsons Close to the junction with Moorcroft Avenue. Turn left, and after 34 yds, having passed the first house on the right and its cypress hedge, turn right down a path across a green swathe with trees. The Avon Valley sign is on the tree trunk. Continue under oak trees through the estate. At Priory View Road, turn left over a stile, keeping to a gravel track beside the road. After 60 yds, pass through a gap in the metal rail on the right and cross the road to the tarmac path. Pass under an arch of trees between houses. Continue to Pittmore Road. Cross the road and follow the path, passing a children's play area over a stream to Stony Lane beside the telephone kiosk. If you become lost, follow any road in an westerly direction to Stony Lane, which is the main road to Christchurch.

Turn left towards Christchurch for 50 yds to a footbridge where the main road crosses the stream from Ripley. Turn right, keeping the stream on the left and cross a stile into the water meadows. Cross to the next stile where there is a notice board with an illustration of the flora and fauna of the Lower Avon water meadows. Heading out across the meadows between the stream and a trig point, head for a board-walk that crosses a small water course; alternatively, head towards the Southbourne Water Tower to the south-west. The path leads to the river bank. Follow the left bank of the river along the raised levee to the weir at the water works. Cross the weir and follow the path to the water works. Walk alongside the east and south walls of the brick pump house.

The path continues to the left between a yew hedge and a portakabin. Continue between two wire fences with the mill tail on the left and the yard for the water works on the right. Pass the point where the mill tail rejoins the river and continue along the river bank past two water pipes that cross the river and head towards the railway bridge over the river.

The path passes to the rear of some houses on the outskirts of Christchurch before it turns away from the river $1/2$ mile from Christchurch Centre, down a narrow lane called Avon Buildings. The lane ends at the main road at Bargates opposite the Royalty Inn. Turn left towards the Priory and the High Street. At the large roundabout, take the underpass under Fountain Way and follow the signs to the tourist information centre to be found on the right before the library on the High Street. Christchurch Priory can be seen at the south end of the High Street. The bus to Ringwood stops outside the Old Town Hall halfway down the High Street.

Section 10
CHRISTCHURCH

Continue along Bargates; the road was named after the north gate to the town which stood in the middle of the High Street until it was removed in 1744.

The existence of the Bargate tells a little of the history of **Christchurch**, which was one of three Hampshire burhs, or fortified towns. Situated at the mouth of the Avon, dominating two rivers, it was first called Tweon-ea or Twin – meaning 'between the waters.' In AD 600 it was occupied by the Saxons; when the shopping centre was built on the corner of Bargate and Fountain Way in 1978, a seventh-century Saxon graveyard was uncovered, containing 34 graves and a Bronze Age barrow mound. It is believed that in AD 700 Alfred the Great built an earth bank round the town in order to protect it from the Vikings who had invaded the Isle of Wight. In AD 876 it is thought that warships known as aescas sheltered in the harbour while watching for the Vikings during the battle at Swanage.

The *Anglo-Saxon Chronicle* recounts that in AD 901 Aethelwold, a nephew of Alfred the Great, attacked Twinham and captured the earth ramparts, but was ultimately defeated. As a result, King Edam the Elder decided to fortify the town with a wooden castle on a motte probably completed in AD 924. Further development at this time was halted in 1006 by the Viking invasion of the town, by then called Thiunam.

At the southern end of the High Street is the Priory, a very fine church dating from 1094 when Ralph Flambard, William Rufus's chief minister, began to replace the old Saxon church with the present building.

Christchurch Priory is a fine example of a medieval monastic church. It is known for being the longest parish church in the country, with a nave over 311 feet long. The nave and transepts were built mostly during the Norman period and have heavy Norman columns and round arches. The lady chapel was built during the more delicate Perpendicular period of the fourteenth century and the great choir was rebuilt during the sixteenth century.

The Priory is famous for the Miraculous Beam, which attracts pilgrims from around the world. It was said that during the construction of the church there was one particular carpenter who noticeably never seemed to take refreshment nor collect his pay. One day a beam was cut too short for its position on the roof; as it was the end of the day it was decided to leave it until the morning. When the men arrived next day they found that the beam was miraculously the right length and in the correct position. The strange carpenter was never seen again and rumour has it that it was none other than the Carpenter of Nazareth.

Christchurch Priory seen from the southern end of the High Street.

From that time the church and town were renamed Cris-charche den Twenham or Cristes-Church.

Whilst in the church, look out for the fine Jesse Screen and visit the St Michael Loft Museum, which was once the Christchurch grammar school. Lessons were often interrupted by the antics of the smugglers returning from Hengistbury Head with their contraband in wagons or concealed about their persons. From the schoolroom and from the top of the tower there is a panoramic view across the harbour. The weather vane on top of the tower was used to warn the smugglers of the whereabouts of the preventive men; the fish, probably a salmon, being turned to point in their direction.

Leaving the church by the magnificent thirteenth-century porch, continue through the West Gate to the road. To the right can be found the Red House Museum, but turning left one passes on the left a small private house, once the porter's lodge, the only remains of the great monastery attached to the Priory church which was destroyed in 1539 by Henry VIII when he gave the church to the town. Continue though the car park to the Town Quay, where the River Avon meets the River Stour and flows into Christchurch Harbour and down to the sea at Mudeford. The quay was once very busy, as the harbour had two tides, making it easier for boats to come in and unload their cargoes. There was hard standing of gravel and ironstone.

The harbour can contain 24 varieties of fish. The waters are tidal and therefore normally salty; however, on calm days the river water remains separate from the denser, heavier salt water and floats on the incoming tide. At these times it is possible to find freshwater roach, dace, gudgeon, barbel, perch and chub near the surface and salt water fish below.

The quay area is also a gathering place for the many swans which frequent the rivers and harbour which are a haven for all birds, especially during the winter months. On the left bank of the harbour is Stanpit Marsh, a 150-acre wetland site which received nature reserve status in 1967. There is also a large area on Hengistbury Head allocated nature reserve status.

Place Mill, on the left of the quay, first mentioned in the Domesday Book, was used by the monastic community at the time of the Dissolution, after which it continued in use, serving the community until its closure in 1908. Today, still owned by Christchurch Corporation, it has been restored and is now open to the public.

Officially the Avon Valley Footpath ends at the Priory Church, so it is best to return, crossing Place Mill Bridge and following the Convent Walk to town. This walk opened in 1911 to commemorate the Coronation of King George V leads along the bank between the mill stream and the river, round the castle to Town Bridge. Today this is an extremely pleasant and popular walk, but this was not always so, as until 1902 all sewage and waste from the slaughter house at Town Bridge were discharged straight into the river. This did not, however, discourage Diner Parsons, who worked at the slaughter house, from celebrating his birthday each year by diving off Town Bridge and swimming in the river.

Both in 1841 and 1855 the river froze and became the scene of much enjoyment. Shops were shut for an hour each day to allow people time to skate or even to ride ponies on the ice. In 1841 a large fire was built and a sheep was roasted on the river. In the balmier days of 1909 there was a regatta in which the church choir dressed as Venetian serenaders sang from a gondola on the river.

There is a fine view of the castle from Convent Walk. Built originally as a wooden fort by Richard de Redvers, cousin to Henry I, in the early twelfth century, it was later rebuilt in a mixture of ironstone from Hengistbury Head and limestone from the Isle of Wight by Baldwin de Redvers to resist King Stephen in his civil war against the Empress Matilda. In 1153, King Stephen captured the castle and took Baldwin prisoner, but he was able to escape and retake it. The castle was not to see action again until the Civil War in 1644.

Throughout its history the castle was visited by most reigning monarchs; King John came at least eight times on his way to Corfe Castle. In the late thirteenth century Edward I fortified the keep with stone, but this failed to prevent the castle falling to the Parliamentarians without a shot being fired in 1644. It is said that at the time the governor of the castle, Sir John Mills, had called a council of war, which enabled the Roundheads not only to capture the castle but to take captive 100 Gentlemen of Position, 400 Infantry and 280 horses. On 15 January 1645, Royalists mounted a counter attack which lasted for three days. Houses on the corner of Church Street and Castle Street were demolished to allow cannon to be mounted for firing. The castle was powerful enough to resist and eventually this was its downfall. Oliver Cromwell, fearing so powerful a stronghold, ordered its destruction in 1652.

In 1160 the **Constable's House** was built with features which must have been considered very luxurious at the time. The house was built on two floors, the bailiff having his living quarters upstairs, where there are large windows and one of the earliest chimneys in the country. There was also a privy or garderobe jutting out over the mill stream.

The river here is divided into two; the western arm is crossed by Town Bridge and the eastern arm by Waterloo Bridge. Town Bridge was once known as Quartley's Bridge after Doctor Quartley who lived at Bridge House. There is a fascinating story associated with Doctor Quartley. One night he was taken on horseback by two masked men to a house in Bransgore, where he found a man lying on the floor suffering from a gunshot wound to his back. The doctor removed the bullet and gave instructions that he should not be moved. It transpired, however, that the man was a young seaman and smuggler called Tom and to stay would mean certain death. Tom was moved and a while later the doctor found a keg of fine brandy at his door. Fifteen years later, while visiting Mr Mills at Bisterne Manor, the party went out after dinner on the river. The boatman/gardener introduced himself to the doctor as the same Tom.

In 1665, when the plague was rampant, watchmen were employed round the clock to stand guard over the bridge and prevent any strangers, especially any Londoners, from entering the town.

Turn left at Castle Street and cross Castle Bridge over the mill stream; almost immediately on the left is an old timber-framed building – now a perfumery – which was once the Court House and dates back to the twelfth century. Courts were held here from the thirteenth century and the property continued in use until 1920 for the swearing-in each year of the mayor and the chief officials of the borough.

The small roundabout where Castle Street meets the High Street marks the site of the Saxon Market Square: the commercial centre of the old town since Christchurch had been granted a Monday market in 1150. In the centre stood

The Old Court House, Christchurch.

the old town hall from 1745 until it was moved to its present position in the High Street in 1858. Sadly, the market bell which hung in the cupola was not reinstated after the move and has since vanished.

Beside the roundabout is the George Inn, which, with the Ship Inn in the High Street, is probably the oldest in Christchurch. The building dates from 1654, when it was the George and Dragon, and stood beside the Market Cross.

Refreshments are good at the George; stop a while and soak up the atmosphere of an old inn with very definite smuggling connections. For many years smuggling was one of Christchurch's most lucrative industries. Although it was illegal, many professional people – doctors, parsons, brewers, bankers and traders – felt that because of the ridiculously high taxes on such items as tea and tobacco, even French gloves, they were morally right to dabble in a little free trading. Thus it became big business during the eighteenth and nineteenth centuries and a vast capital was invested by many of the town's leading citizens. They were able to accumulate great wealth, and much of this was left to the townspeople in the form of charitable gifts. Ellis Coffin, who was a seafaring man and a resident of Mudeford, bequeathed in his will a house and shop (now occupied by Lloyds Bank) with the express intention that all the rental income from the premises should be shared amongst the poor of the town at Christmas each year. There are several instances of charitable donations to the poor of the town and many continue to this day.

There were few ports so suitable for smuggling as Christchurch. It is surrounded by gently shelving beaches, and apart from Christchurch Ledges, there are no rocks. The harbour has two tides and there was a quay where heavy goods could be unloaded. The routes inland were good, with an excellent network of paths leading across the inhospitable heathland all around to Cranborne Chase, Bath and Bristol and across the New Forest to London. In winter the two rivers, the Stour and the Avon would flood, effectively sealing off the town. The position of the town was important, too, being at the centre of two bays, Bournemouth and Poole Bay and Christchurch Bay. It was also close to the French coast, the Channel Isles and even to Holland.

The history of smuggling dates back at least to the early years of the reign of Queen Elizabeth I, when young Roman Catholics were smuggled to France for their education and Catholic religious books were smuggled into this country. The heyday, however, was from 1760 to 1820, when the American War of Independence and the Seven Years War leading to the Napoleonic Wars caused all trade with France to cease and heavy taxes to be levied. At this time silk, cloth, lace, soap, tobacco, spirits, pearls, cards, gloves and tea were all items of contraband and, curiously, there was a demand for French dolls dressed in the latest fashions. During the French Revolution in 1790 there was a trade in French refugees; aristocrats who were seeking safety in England. Their rendezvous was often Beech House in Bransgore.

Tea, which was often hidden between ships' timbers disguised as flooring, was carried by the bearers about their bodies after it was landed. It is said that a man could carry as much as 18 pounds in his trousers or up to 30 pounds in his hat, waistcoat or in a woman's bustle, for women were used both as bearers and look outs. Custom records for 1764 show that the East India Company smuggled in 7 million pounds of tea that year.

Tobacco was coiled into rope or hidden in casks of bones being imported to make glue. It is of interest that John Streeter of Mudeford, owner of a lug-sail boat, the *Phoenix*, who made regular runs for brandy, was known as the respected owner of a snuff factory at Stanpit. It is thought that Napoleon also used English smugglers as his fifth column for moving gold and for carrying out spying missions.

No. 10 Bridge Street was the headquarters of the Customs and Excise and home of their most loyal and trustworthy supervisor, Abraham Pike. As well as being supervisor for the coastal area between Poole and Hurst Castle, he was also a coast waiter who supervised the unloading of the luggers at the quay and chief riding officer. From 1795, when the barracks were built, he was supported by the Dragoons under the command of L.D.G. Tregonwell, who was to become known as the founder of Bournemouth, when he acquired 8 acres of cliff top and heath and built Exeter House.

Gradually smuggling went into decline when the Napoleonic Wars ended in 1815. Hundreds of Royal Naval ships and their crews were released from military service and were used to wage war instead upon the smugglers. In 1831 the coastguard service was established at Haven House, Mudeford, and in 1861 the coastguard cottages were built overlooking the run and the harbour, effectively ending the illegal traded.

We have now reached the end of the Avon Valley Footpath, and it is time to reflect upon all that we have seen and learnt along the way. Geographically we have walked from the high chalk land of Wiltshire, through the gravel heathlands of the New Forest in Hampshire, to the water meadows and harbour in Dorset. On our pilgrimage we have passed from Salisbury Cathedral, the centre of the Diocese of Salisbury, through land held by the Diocese of Winchester to the Priory of Christchurch, given to the town by Henry VIII. Historically we have seen the remains of early Britons at Downton, and all along the way evidence of the middle ages, the Tudors and the industrial age. Such variety was made accessible to us by the hard work and commitment of local ramblers' organisations, with the assistance of Hampshire County Council and the support of both Wiltshire and Dorset County Councils. Let us hope that we continue to have access to our inland waterways for many generations to come.

FURTHER READING

John Ashley-Cooper, *A Ring of Wessex Water*, H.F. & G. Witherby

John Baker, *A Picture of Hampshire*, Hale, 1986, SHLC

Nancy Bell, *From Harbour to Harbour, 1916*

John Chandler, *Endless Street,* Hobnob Press, 1988

Donald A.E. Cross, *The Story of Ringwood's Industries*, 1963, SHLC

Ken Davies, *New Forest Airfields,* Niche Publishing, 1992

G. M. Dear, *From Watermills to Waterworks in Christchurch,* 1979

Celia Fiennes, *The Journey of Celia Fiennes,* 1947

F. Hardcastle, *Records of Burley,* Chameleon International, 1950, revised 1987

H. Colt Hoare, *History of Modern Wiltshire*

R.L.P. Jowitt, *Salisbury*, Batsford, 1951

Capt. Hon. Rupert Keppel, *The Ringwood Story Part II*, 1960

K. Merle Chacksfield, *Smuggling Days*, Christchurch Times, 1966

K. Merle Chacksfield, *The Dorset and Somerset Rebellion*, Dorset Publishing, 1985

William Cobbett, *Rural Rides,* 1830

Richard Mabey and T. Evans, *The Flowering of Britain*, Hutchinson, 1980

The New Forest Book, ed. by James O'Donald Mays, 1989, SLHC

D.H. Montray Read, *Highways and Byways in Hampshire*

A.T. Morley-Hewitt, *Story of Fordingbridge in Fact and Fancy, 1965*

Geoffrey Morley, *Smuggling in Hampshire and Dorset, 1700-1850*, Countryside Books, 1983

Sam Morris, *A Glimpse of Sopley*, 1989, SLHC

Richard and Nina Muir, *Fields*, Macmillan, 1989

Noreen O'Dell, *The River Avon*, Paul Cave, 1991

Kingsley Palmer, *Oral Folk Tales of Wessex*, David and Charles,1973

Nikolaus Pevsner, *Dorset*, Penguin Books,1972

Nikolaus Pevsner and David Lloyd, *Hampshire*, Penguin Books, 1967

Nikolaus Pevsner, *Wiltshire*, Penguin Books, 1975

E.H. Lane Poole, *Damerham and Martin*, Compton Russel Ltd, 1986

Francis Price, *A Series of Particular and Useful Observations upon that Admirable Structure the Cathedral Church of Salisbury*, R. Baldwin, 1753

The Victoria County History of Wiltshire, Vol 6, ed. B Pugh, 1900

Olive J. Samuel, *On the Bridge*

City of Salisbury, ed. Hugh Short, Phoenix House, 1957

Heywood Sumner, *Ancient Earthworks of Cranborne Chase,* Chiswick Press, 1913

Heywood Sumner, *Wessex*, re-issued, Roy Gasson Associates, 1985

Brian Vesey Fitzgerald, *Avon Valley, 1950*

Sidney Vines, *English Chalk Streams*, Batsford, 1992

Allen White, *Christchurch through the Years*, SLHC, 1985

Brian J. Woodruffe, *Wiltshire Villages*, Hale, 1982

Geoffrey N. Wright, *Roads and Trackways of Wessex*, Moorland, 1988

E.M. Clelland and Pat Hall, *Woodgreen, Village without Title*

INDEX

NOTES